Anne Liberty

21 Easy Macramé Projects for Beginners and Advanced Step by Step Illustrated

Author: Anne Liberty

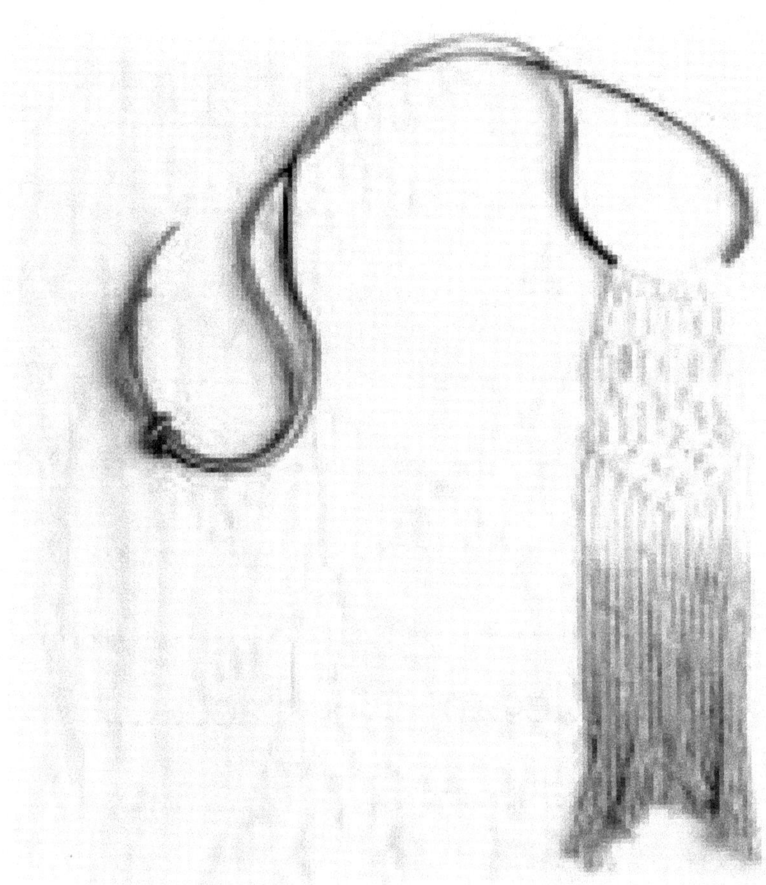

Table of Contents

Introduction

Macramé is a way of creating textiles that uses knots rather than weaving or knitting techniques. Macramé has often been used by sailors to decorate objects or their ships and is also used to make jewelry, bags, mats, plant hooks and wall hangings. Sometimes leather and suede are used to make macramé belts, and macramé is used to create friendship bracelets made by many children.

There is a wide range of knots and knot combinations used in macramé including a square knot, a half knot, a half knot, a lark head knot and a coil knot. Depending on the knots used and whether they are used alone or in combination with others, many different designs can be achieved. When choosing which material to use for a project, it is important to think about what the finished item is and how it will be used as some will be more practical or appropriate than others. Often rigid, thick cords are not the best choice for jewelry making, but they could be ideal for a shopping bag that needs to carry some weight and not fry or wear easily. If several types of cords are suitable for a project, they may result in quite different finished objects. The design of a bracelet made of fine cotton cord will be softer, lighter and more discreet than the same piece made of a thicker leather cord, for example. Another thing to consider in relation to the thickness of the ropes is how easy they will be to use. Thicker cords may be easier, but some types of knots are difficult to keep in place when they are thick. Thin cords can be faithful and slow to work with, but the results can be stunning and very detailed.

Beads are often added to the embellishment of macramé products. Again, the ones you chose will need to be suitable for the cord being used and to fit the function of the finished piece. Wooden beads are a common choice, but there is no reason why any other type with a hole large enough to accommodate ropes should not be used. Other items, such as buttons, sequins and charms, may also be used.

Findings of many types of items or other items may be needed to complete the design and make it possible for them to be used. Examples of items you may use are ear wires, clasps, buckles, snap hooks, split rings, bamboo rings, and buttons.

Macramé as an aspect of decorative knots permeates nearly every culture, but within those cultures, it can manifest in different directions. The carefully braided strings, with the assistance of a needle-like tool, became the item for shaping fishnets. Their use in the fashion industry has been spectacular and influential among the youth in making sandals, shoes, jewelry, etc. It is now used also with other products to fashion all kinds of beautiful works of art.

Macramé is closely associated with the trendy youth due to its rapid growth, quick adaptability, and extensive uses. Concerning its use for fashion items, macramé exercised in the textiles became an essential focus on the creation of each decorative piece of clothing, particularly on the fringes of each tent, clothing, and towel. In this, macramé became a synonym for hanging planter. In its traditional forms, Macramé (is an Italian name given in Genoa-its home and place of birth) became one of the most common textile techniques.

Knots are used for the passage of time for several practical, mnemonic and superstitious reasons. Knotting dates back to early Egyptian civilization in Africa, where knots were used in fishnet and decorative fringes. The Peruvian Incas used a Quip, made from mnemonic knot (Basically, overhand knots) to help them record and convey information. The use of ties, the knot size, rope color, and knot both helped to communicate complicated messages Knots were used in surgery (as slings for broken bones) and in games in ancient Greece (one such mystery was the Gordian knot). In the early Egyptians and Greek times,' Hercules ' knot (square knot) was used on clothes, jewelry, and pottery, which had a spiritual or religious meaning.

There is a wide range of colors, textures and types of cords available for use in macramé, some natural and some synthetic. In fact, almost anything you can tie knots in will be appropriate and materials can be found in a number of locations, such as: craft, hardware, DIY, needlework and sewing shops. In some cases, the material used will be dictated by what is being created, but in others, it may be possible to experiment with your own choices, and although there are strings that are commonly used in some projects, this does not mean that others will not work just as well. Some examples of cords that can be used in macramé include:

- Rayon
- Nylon
- Silk
- Waxed
- cotton
- Hemp Plastic
- Polypropylene
- Leather
- Suede

- Wool
- Embroidery thread
- Crochet thread

The near association between contemporary crafts and macramé has led to the discovery of a range of methodologies and integrative methods, common in most cases, in the content and the adapted techniques. Such advanced methods and integrative techniques reflect the accomplishment of macramé art and its development.

Terms used in Macramé

While macramé has become quite a popular art, in some patterns there are still many words and abbreviations that people may not be aware of or may not know the meaning of. I have put together a series of these that can be used to help understand these words and make it easier to interpret macramé patterns.

Alternating– Attach a knot to one cord and then move to tie another cord to the same knot.

ASK– Alternating knots of the square. This abbreviation is often used in macramé patterns because square knots are commonly used.

Band– A long and smooth piece of macramé.

Bar– A set of knots in the design that create an elevated position.

Bight– A small folded cord portion that is forced through the knot.

Body– You're working on the main of the project.

Braid– Braids are sometimes also known as plaits and are formed to loop around each other by connecting three or four cords.

Braided cord– A type of cord consisting of several thinner pieces of cord woven together. Twisted cords tend to be more durable than twisted cords.

Bundles– A series of cords that have been stored.

Knot button– A tight, round decorative knot.

BH– The button's door. Vertical lark head nodes are used to create a loop that could be used for fastening or joining parts.

Chinese Macramé– Knotted designs from China and other countries in Asia.

Crown knot – A decorative knot in Macramé, often called the Chinese flower or Shamrock knot because it looks like a flower when finished.

Combination knot– To create a new type of knot or design feature, use two or more knots.

Cords– Cords is any fiber material that is used to build projects with macramé.

Core– The cord / s running through a project's center and knotting around it. These are sometimes referred to as fillers or main strings.

Crook– The curved part of a cord loop.

Diagonal– A line or row of knots extending from top right to bottom (or vice versa) Diagonal knots such as half-hitch knots are often used in macramé designs.

Diameter– The width usually in millimeters of a cord.

DDH – Half hitch double. This concept of macramé means connecting two knots of half-hitch to each other.

Fillers– cords that remain at the core of a pattern and are knotted around it. Also referred to as core cords.

Findings– objects and fastenings other than cords that can be used to construct loops, fasteners and other functional objects or decorations in macramé designs. There are examples of ear wires and clasps.

Finishing knot– A knot tied to secure the ends of the cord and to prevent them from unravelling.

Fringe– Cord ends lengths not knotted but left suspended.

Knots of fusion– Another term for knots of combination.

Gusset– A term used to design a 3D project's sides like a bag.

Hitch– A knot commonly used to tie cords to other items.

Cord knotting– the cord used in a design to tie the knots.

LH– Knot of the head of larks.

Loop– The circular or oval shape created by the crossing of two parts of a cord.

Micro-Macramé– Macramé projects made using materials that are delicate or small in diameter.

Mount– An object that is used as part of a macramé project, such as a brace, frame or handle. For example: cords mounted on wooden handles at the beginning of a project with a macramé bag.

Natural– Generally this term is used to refer to cords and refers to any material made from plants, wood and other natural substances such as hemp and cotton.

Netting– A series of knots with open spaces between them. Netting is often used to build things like bags and hangers for plants.

OH– Knot overhand.

Picot– Loops on the sides of a design that stand out. These are seen more often in early trends.

Plait– Cords are plated in an alternating pattern by crossing three or more. Also referred to as a braid.

Scallops– Knots loops created along the edges of the design of a macramé.

Segment– Common knot, cord or design areas.

Seniti– This term, also known as a sonnet, is a single chain of identical knots.

Standing end– The cord end was secured on a macramé board or other surface and did not build knots.

SK– Square knot– A common knot created by attaching two cords to one or more cords.

Stitch– Stitch is sometimes used instead of knot in early patterns.

Synthetic – Man-made fibers such as polypropylene and nylon.

Vertical– from top to bottom to top.

Vintage– A pattern, knot, or technique popular in or earlier in the early 1900s. Some vintage knots and patterns are still being used unchanged in macramé today, although others have evolved or disappeared.

Weaving– Weaving cords means placing them under each other or over each other.

Working cord– Another term used to knot cord. The cord with which you are currently working.

Others are;

Fibers-Different writers and projects will use different words to describe knotting material, such as threads, ropes, ropes or strands. Again, this is to prevent the writing and reading of the project from becoming very repetitive, but it all means the same thing: the length of the fiber you're using.

Active and inactive-You can find the terms active and inactive string used when following macramé projects. Active cord refers to the cords that are used to tie the knots, and the inactive ones are not. Whether or not a string is active while creating a design.

Regrouping-Groups of two, three or four strings are used in many macramé projects. Regrouping is a term used to describe the process of joining cords from two adjacent groups. For example, if two groups of two cords are used, the middle two cords will be joined.

Alternating–Alternating is a process of typing a number of rows of knots that are alternately spaced in the design. Alternating can be used to join many groups of strings while still leaving gaps and spacing between knots instead of creating one solid piece of fabric.

Anchoring–Macramé knots are much easier to tie, especially at the beginning of the piece, if they are taut. You can do this by mounting the threads in some way. A slip knot is often used to attach threads to a solid surface as it is an easy knot to disconnect once the project has been completed. Another method is to use pins to secure the strings on the knotting board.

Sennit–Sennit is a length of two or more knots of a single type. For example, if a pattern says you should tie a sennit of five square knots, it means you should tie five square knots one after the other. Sennit is sometimes spelt as a sinnet, too.

Knotting boards

Macramé knotting boards can be bought or made in a number of ways. A simple board can be made using a normal clipboard; the strings are secured under a large clip. Another way to make a simple board is to use a cork notice board and pins. Thick cork tiles could also be used the same way. Some commercially available boards are marked with measurements that are a useful feature. If you decide to make your own board, you can easily add it using a ruler and a permanent marker.

Using a macramé board creates a place for anchoring your cords while working and also makes storing and transporting projects easier. The board can be slipped into a bag and transported easily.

Managing cord lengths

Macramé projects often involve the use of many long cord lengths, which can be knotted and entangled in each other during operation. To avoid this, ropes can be bundled up or wound around themselves and loosely knotted to create a manageable length. As you work through the project, you can untie the knot and release more strings before you retied it. The ropes can also be secured using rubber bands rather than knots.

Another way to make long cord lengths more manageable is to use small spools known as bobbins.

They can easily be bought online by the names ' macramé bobbin' or' Kumihimo bobbins.' The cords are wrapped around them and secured, leaving a length to work with. As this length is used, more cord can easily be released from the coil.

The Basics of Macramé

There are some direct Macramé basics that you'll need to know to start you off. The surer you are about the system of Macramé, the better time you'll have as you complete one project after another. Figuring out the total cording to use:

You'll need to determine to what degree the length of your cording should be. Yet most endeavors will give you the endorsed estimations, you should have some idea of how this estimation is reached. The pieces of the deals are 3 to several times longer than the piece you mean to make, in any case, since the cording is duplicated down the center for knotting. It is assessed at 7 times longer than the whole amount needed.

For example: if the Macramé project will have an ended length of 1 yard, you'll need to measure your cording at 7 to 8 yards starting with one end then onto the next. By then when each end is increased for knotting it will be two ends, each end being 3 ½ to 4 yards long. Guarantee that you measure the completions liberally since you would incline toward not to miss the mark on cording and need to add to the project. It's much better to have extra cording than it is to run out and remember an unbalanced spot for the procedure.

Making a sampler before you start:

You 're going to have to make a sampler for some Macramé ventures with the aim that you too can see how the string knots are measured and how long. Strong cording can take more time of knotting than durable ones, so that you can test how much cording you need to use to account for this. Create a sampler that measures around 3 inches by 6 inches in order to test the length of the cord in a similar way to see what number of ends the model would require for the distance.

Counting beads and other things:

Beads and other things are regularly added to Macramé's projects to make them captivating, unique and rich in ideas. You can buy beads of all kinds from beading and workmanship stores, as well as from various wholesalers on the Internet. All you need to do is ensure that the gaps in the beads seem to be large enough for the cord to be strung through with no problem at all. You simply slide the beads on the cord between or in knots to incorporate the beads.

Precisely when you're adding beads to a job, you'll need to scan for beads that are noteworthy and interesting with the objective that they stand out in the Macramé plan. You'll find beads in a collection of styles, sizes, and shapes that consolidates blooms, pictures, and charms. Look for beads that will enhance the Macramé plan that you're working on. You'll need to pick beads with a covering and surface that are going to update your endeavor.

For smaller exercises you'll need to use beads that are sensitive and delicate while your greater Macramé assignments will need colossal, ended beads. Take as much time as is needed to hunt for the right beads for your endeavor and set out to try other things with new musings.

Summer Sunrise Earrings

Celebrating summer with another fun, original Micro Macrame design. These cheerful earrings offer a fresh look by mixing Chinese Coral C-Lon cord with pearl and iridescent beads.

The cord work segment measures about 1 1/4 inches.

Knots Used:

- Lark's Head Knot
- Flat Knot (aka square knot)
- Double Half Hitch Knot

Supplies:

- C-Lon cord, 2 ft, x 10 (5 cords per earring)
- 2 antique gold jump rings
- 1 set antique gold ear wires
- 8 - 3 mm pearl beads
- 4 - 5 mm apricot beads
- 48 - size 11 iridescent peach beads
- Beacon 527 glue
- wax paper (optional)

Instructions:

Take one cord and place the ends together. Thread both through a 5 mm apricot bead, leaving a loop peeking out of the bead at one end. Place the loose ends of the cord through this open loop as shown. Attach the remaining cords, two per side using Lark's Head (LH) knots.

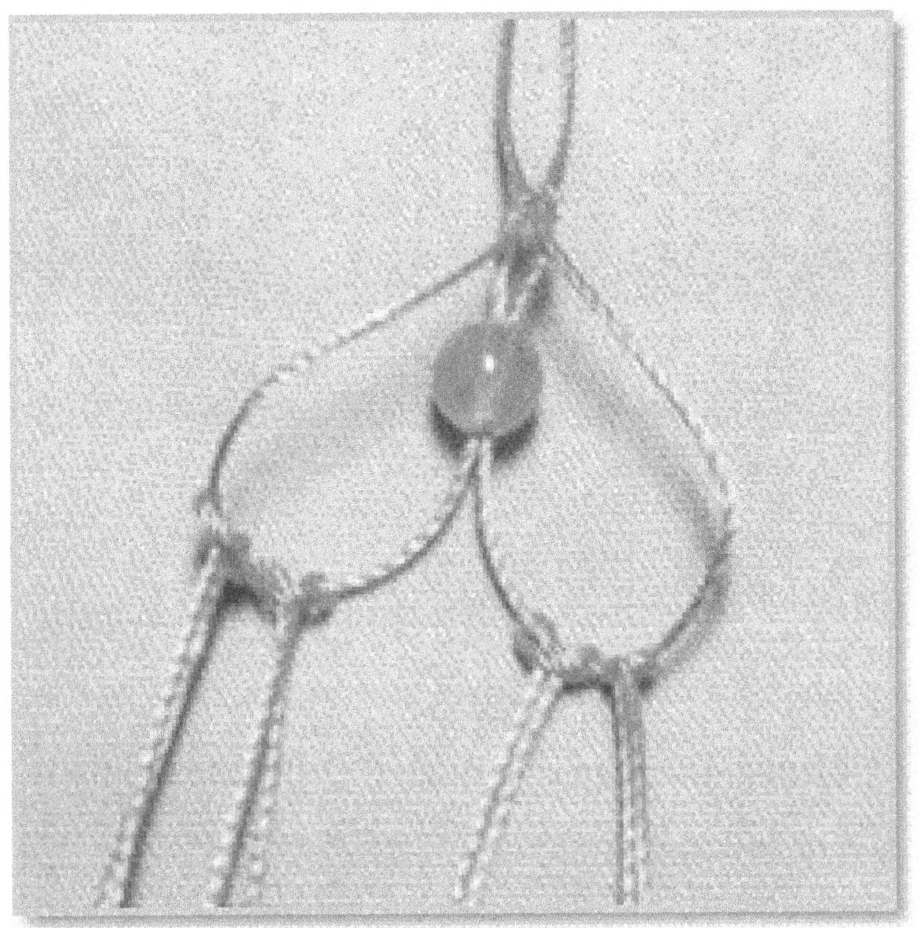

Tighten everything up. Now turn it upside down and pin onto your work surface, separating cords 5-5.

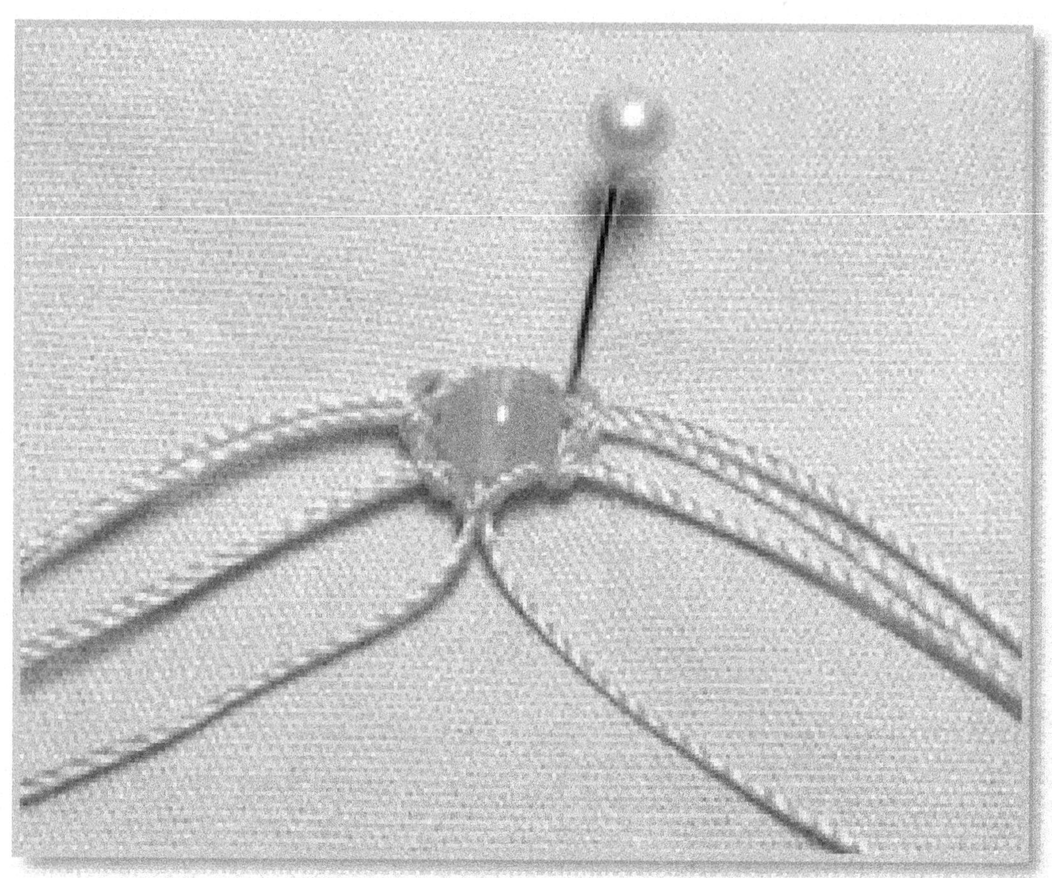

Left 5:

Gently tighten the LH knots. Find the outer left cord. Thread on a size 11 peach seed bead, then place this cord down and to the right as the Holding Cord (HC). Tie Diagonal Double Half Hitch (DDHH) knots onto it with the other 4 cords (outside to inside).

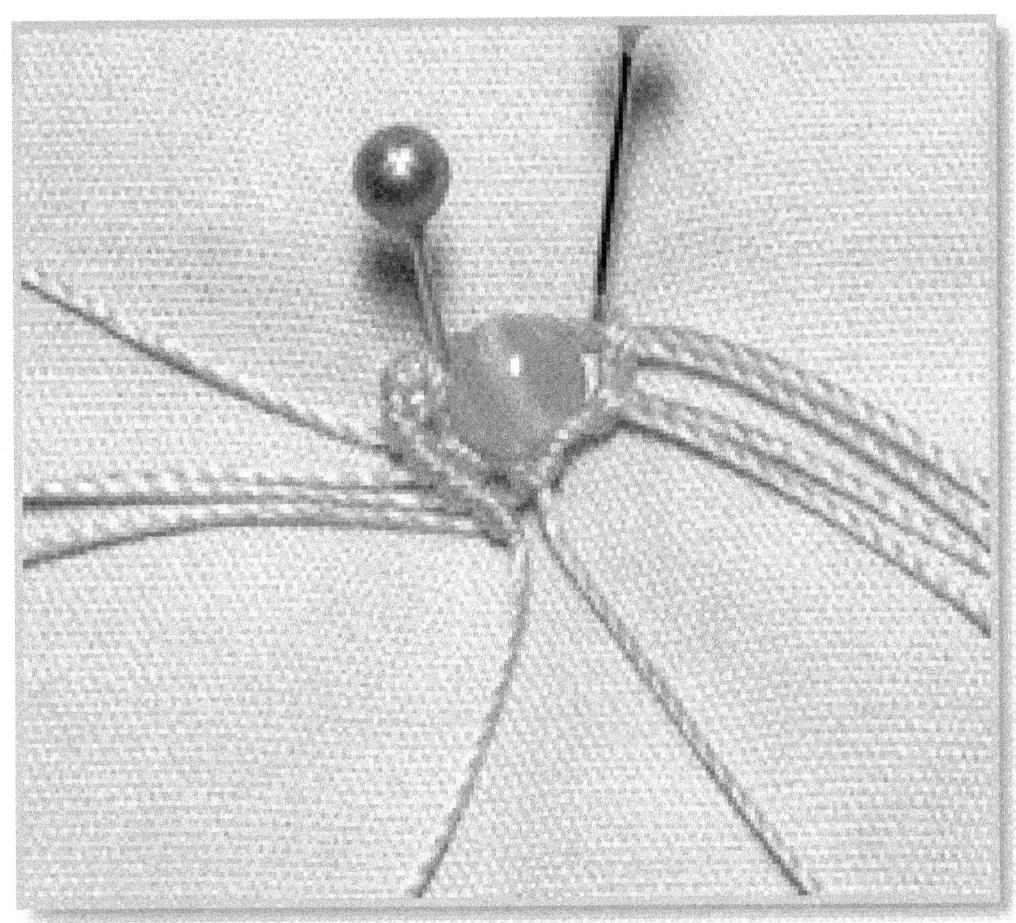

Repeat 2 more times.

Right 5:

Tighten LH knots. Find the outer right cord. Thread on a size 11 peach seed bead, then place this cord down and to the left as the HC. Tie DDHH knots onto it with the other 4 cords (outside to inside). Repeat 2 more times.

Thread a seed bead, a 3mm pearl bead and another seed bead onto each outer cord.

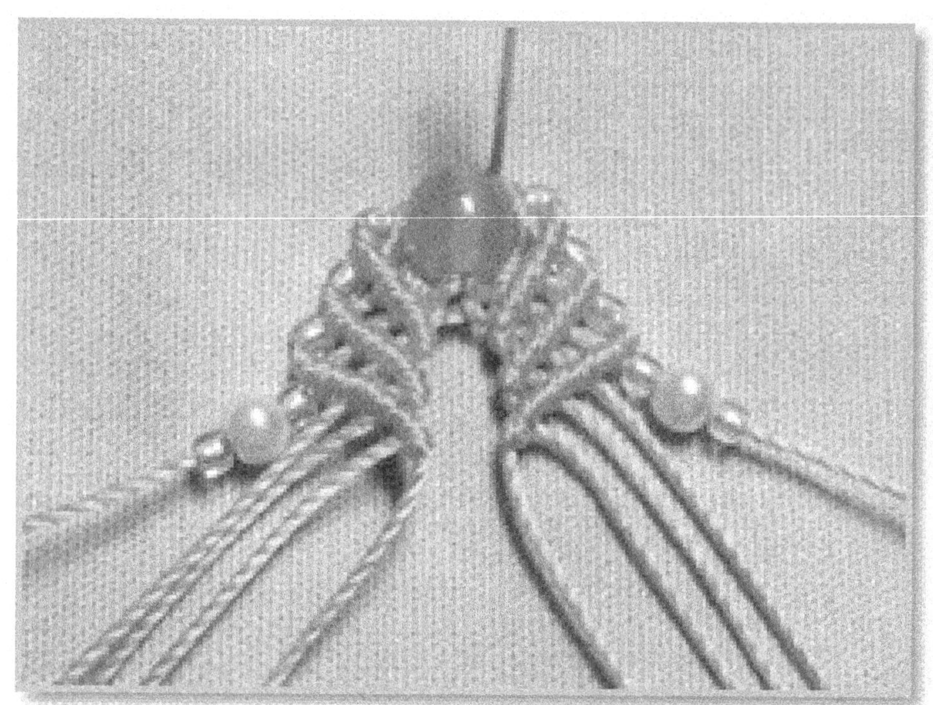

Find the center 2 cords. Place a 3mm pearl bead on each cord. Take a 5mm apricot bead and thread one cord in from each side.

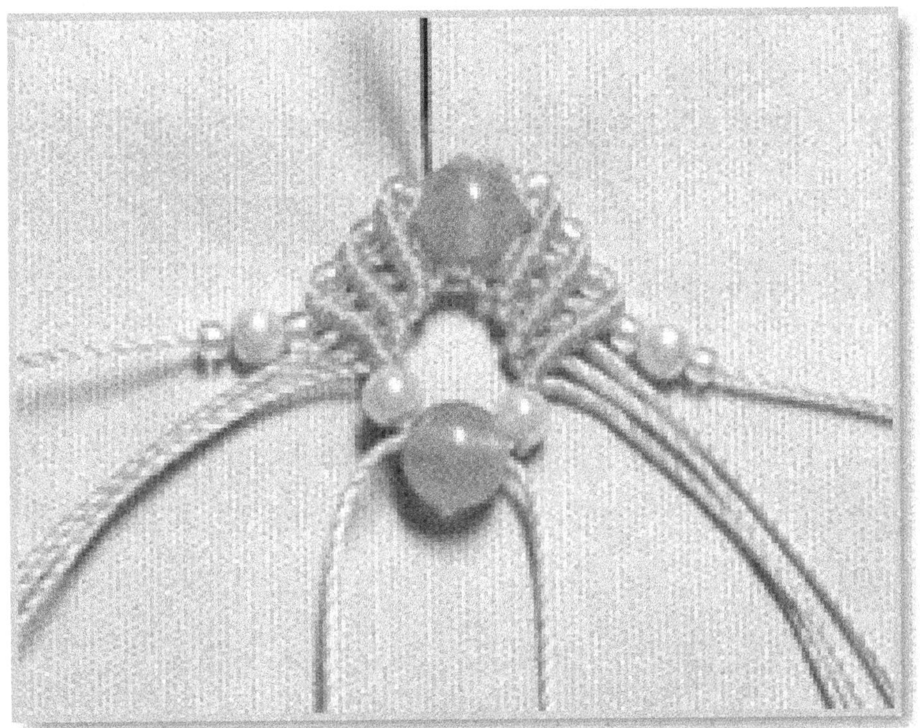

From the center, find the following cord out on the left and place on it 7 seed beads. Repeat with the following cord out (from the center) on the right.

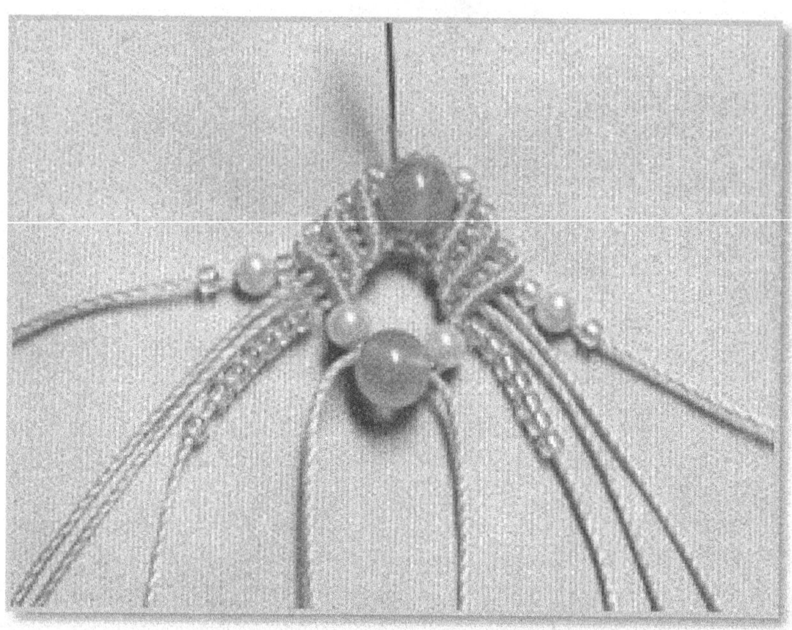

Now use these two beaded cords to tie a flat knot around the inner 2 cords, tightening up and being mindful of bead placement.

With left 3 cords:

Using the outer left cord as the Wrapping Cord (WC), tie 10 DHH knots around the other 2 cords to form a bundle.

With right 3 cords:

Using the outer right cord as the WC, tie 10 DHH knots around the other 2 cords to form a bundle. Bend each of the bundles so they curve inward slightly.

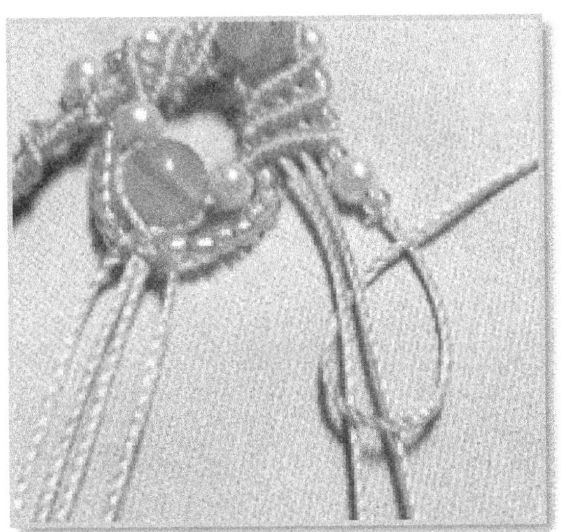

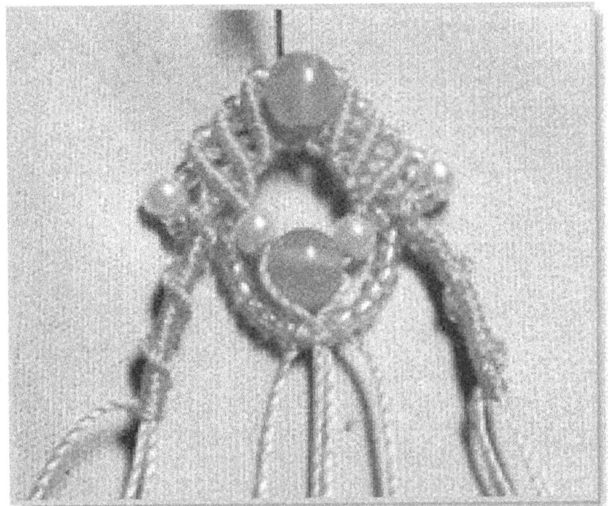

Place all the cords together and tie a flat knot with the outer 2 cords, then put all the cords except the outer most on each side, through a jump ring.

Now turn it right-side up, then flip to the back. Gather all the cords that are through the jump ring and place them straight down.

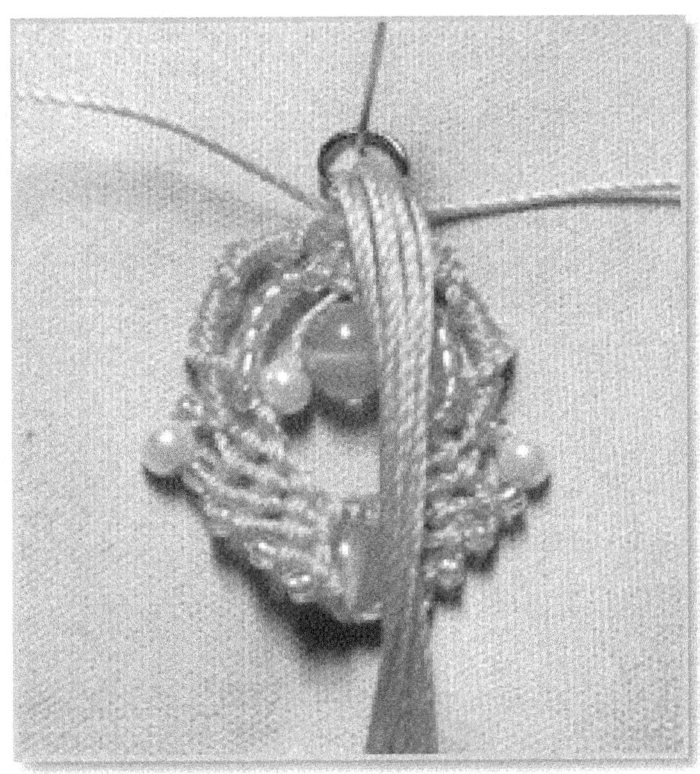

Tie a flat knot with the outer 2 cords around all others.

Glue, trim, glue again. I usually sandwich the piece between layers of wax paper to avoid getting glue where I don't want it.

Place the jump ring on an earring wire, then repeat the pattern to create its mate.

Owl

For this project you will need: The different colored threads as shown above. Eye beads, one nose bead and a sitting pole for the owl. The threads will be referred to by color and the shorter pink thread will be called the short pink thread. You may need some pins to hold down your work throughout.

Step 1: Take both of the short pink threads and tie an overhand knot on the right end of the threads as shown.

Step 2: Take both threads, now form a loop on top of the thread. This can be done by using your thumb as a guide to how long the loop should be. Then hold the thread at this length so that the loop is isolated.

Step 3: Whilst keeping the loop isolated, create another loop with the rest of the threads and then place the original loop through the new loop while keeping hold of the original loop and then when through you can pull to tighten and you should end up with something like the picture above.

Step 4: Take your black thread and lay it down horizontally below the pink thread as shown here. You can pin the thread down to give you more stability for the steps ahead. Some people really find this helpful.

Step 5: Take one of the pink threads and fold it in half. Place it behind the black and short pink threads that are already in place.

Step 6: A loop should have been created at the top of your pink thread. Fold this over the black and short pink threads. Now pull the end of the pink thread

through the loop and pull tightly to secure. This will create a Lark's head knot (image above).

Step 7: Take one of your blue threads and create a Lark's head knot in the same way as earlier shown. Make sure they are subsequent to each other. If the step is followed correctly it should look like the image above.

Step 8: Take three more blue threads and create three more Lark's head knots making sure you have two each side of the knot in the middle. The pink knot just created will act as the middle knot so you will already have a blue on the right.

Step 9: After this is completed, take two pink threads and create a Lark's Head knot on the right and one on the left like in the image above.

Step 10: For this step you will need to create two more overhand knots on the ends of the Lark's head knots.

Step 11: Firstly, do this on the left side ensuring that the Lark's head knot is secured by the overhand knot.

Step 12: Now repeat this for the right-hand side. You can refer back to the prior instructions.

TIP: when creating the overhand knots make sure you do not tighten the knot until it gets down to the Lark's head knot then tighten to secure.

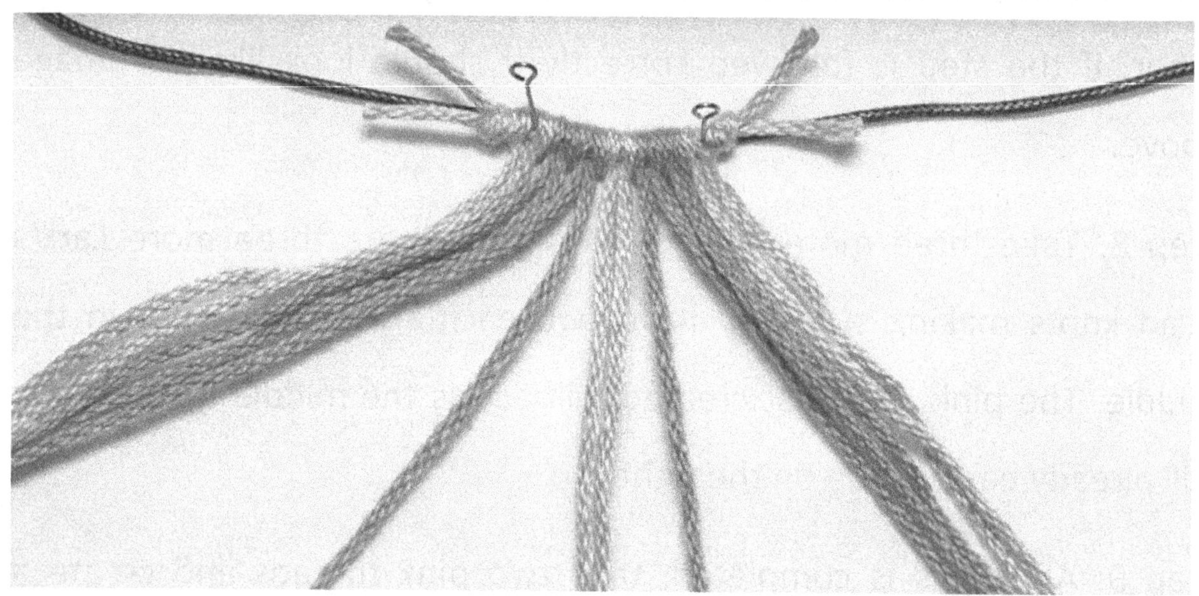

Otherwise you will end up with a knot in the middle of your thread.

Step 13: Trim the ends of the thread left after creating the over hand knots. Make sure to leave around an inch of thread like the picture shows.

Step 14: Starting from the left, take two pink threads and three blue threads and pull them aside.

Step 15: Starting from the right take two pink threads and three blue threads and pull them to the right. After completing this you should have the threads left that are in the image. This should be two pink threads in the middle and one blue either side.

Step 16: At this stage, ignore the five threads either side and focus on the four threads in the middle that you indicated earlier.

Step 17: Take the left blue thread, place over the two pink threads and under the single blue thread on the right. Now take the right blue thread and place it under the pink threads and through the loop created by the blue threads. Simultaneously pull both blue threads and push the knot upwards to secure the knot in place. You can also pull the pink threads down to ensure they are hanging free. You will have created a half square knot.

Step 18: Starting from the right group of threads which consists of five threads. Skip the first thread on the right and proceed to create a half square knot as in the instructions above.

Step 19: Now go to the left side group of threads. Skip the first thread on the left and use the remaining four threads to, again, create a half square knot and your macramé piece should look like the above.

Step 20: Proceed to create two half square knots under your three half square knots prior made and then create a single half square knot under your two. It should look like the image above. The instructions to follow are above.

Step 21: Separate your threads into two groups so that there is 7 in each one (4 blue, 3 pink).

Step 22: Firstly, for your left group of threads take the first pink thread at the top and place it diagonally across your left group of threads. Then take the thread subsequent to it and follow the instructions below.

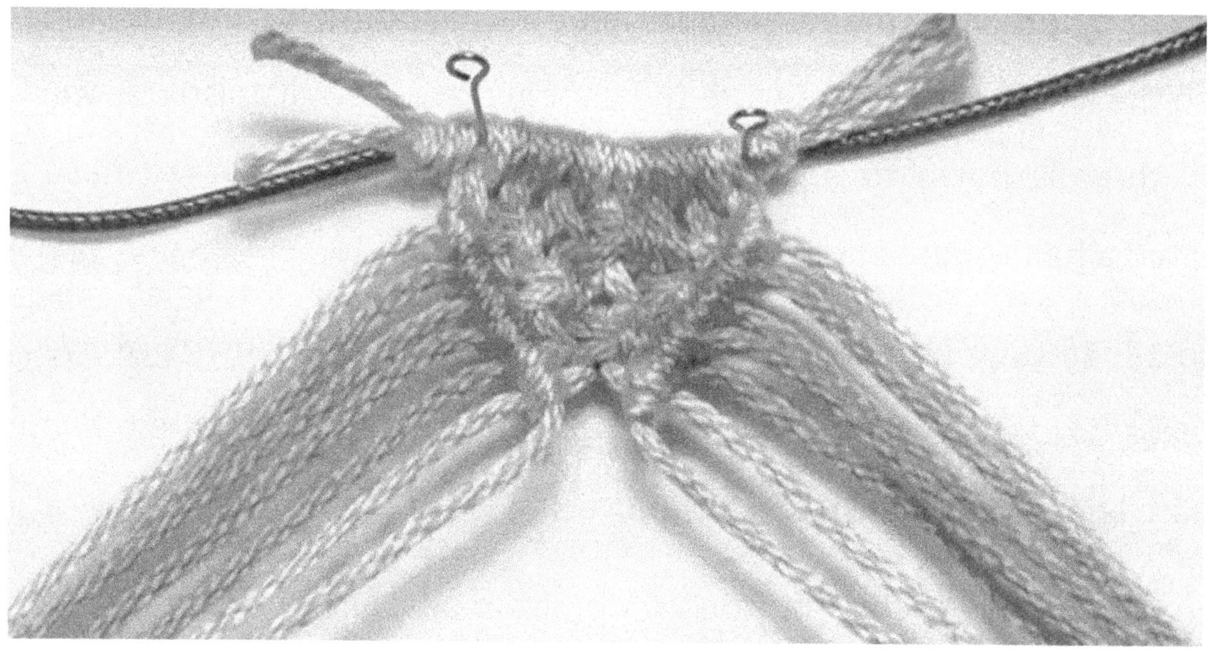

Step 23: Loop it over the horizontal thread, under itself, then using the same thread loop it over the horizontal thread again and finally through the loop created. Pull to secure the knot tightly. You will have a half hitch knot.

Step 24: Now take the first pink thread on the right, place it diagonally across the group of threads. Take the thread following to it and repeat the steps above on how to create a half hitch knot.

Step 25: Your threads should still be separated into two groups. From the group on the left take the first pink thread on the top, the blue thread subsequent to it and use the pink thread to create 5 half hitch knots on the blue thread. Your image should look like the image below.

This is what the left side of your work should look like as this point.

Step 26: Here, proceed to complete a half hitch knot in the same way as described above but on the right side. Instructions above.

Step 27: Now, on the right side subsequent to your half hitch knot, take the three blue threads and pass them through one of the eye beads and push all the way to the top.

Step 28: Repeat this for the three blue threads on the left as well. Your macramé piece should look like the picture shown.

Step 29: Take a new pink thread from your pile. Put it through the nose bead so that the nose bead is in the middle. Then hover the thread over the piece making sure the nose bead is in the middle and then place down.

Step 30: Once you have the new thread horizontally on the piece. Take the first pink thread on the right and tie a half hitch knot around the horizontal pink thread.

TIP: For now, it is okay that the nose bead if not in the same place. It will come back into place in the process.

Step 31: After tying the first half hitch knot with the pink thread, take the subsequent blue threads and tie a single half hitch knot using each one. Then proceed to take the succeeding two pink threads and tie a half hitch knot in each one.

Step 32: Before proceeding, ensure that the nose bead is in the middle and is placed exactly where you would like it. Now proceed to create a series of half hitch knots on the eight side. This should then look like the image below.

Step 33: If you pinned the work down earlier you can take them out as your work should be stable enough as we proceed.

If you completed the steps as told you should end up with your work looking like this. Your owl should be coming along nicely.

Step 34: Below your nose bead in the middle you should have a pink thread on each side. Take the one on the left and place horizontally across the threads on the left. Tie half hitch knots from right to left inclusive of all threads on the left.

Step 35: Secondly, repeat this for the right side.

Step 36: On each side of the Owl's nose bead there should be two half hitch knots.

Step 37: Take the 4 threads in the middle which consists of two pink in the middle and one blue either side. Now tie a half square knot using these threads.

Step 38: Use the prior instructions on how to create this knot.

Step 39: Now, take the succeeding four threads on the left of the half square knot just created in the middle and create another half square knot. Then repeat this process for the right-hand side. It should look like the picture above.

Step 40: Proceed to create more square knots under the ones just created so that you have three on the outer part of the owl. Below this create a row of only two square knots. Then below this one creates on square knot below the two.

Step 41: Go back up the nose of your owl and look down to the half hitch knots. The second ones on the left and right will have a common thread running through them that also goes out past the knots and extends horizontally.

Step 42: From both the threads, attach 3 threads to the left one, using a lark's head knot. Out of the 3 threads you attached 2 should be blue and 1 pink. Make sure you arrange as seen in the picture above, as their arrangement is going to be the start of the wings of the owl.

Step 43: From the wing of the owl, take a single pink thread from the right and place it horizontally across your threads and take the thread subsequent to it and create a half hitch knot(loop the thread over the horizontal one twice and pull through the loop tightly to secure the knot). Repeat this with each thread from the left to right till your work looks like the image above.

Step 44: Now take the last pink thread and create another half hitch knot, as seen in the image above.

Step 45: Below our preceding half hitch knot, take the first thread on the right and place it horizontally across your other threads and take thread to the horizontal thread and create a half hitch knot, repeat for all the other threads on that row of threads.

Step 46: Continue creating rows of half hitch knots until you have 7 rows of them (the half hitch knots should progressively become more vertical as you go along. This is supposed to happen).

Step 47: Now simply repeat what you have done on the right wing on the left wing.

If you have followed the steps correctly your work should look like the image above.

Now that you have completed both wings, you are going to join the wings to the body of the owl.

Step 48: From the group of threads located on the body of the owl, split the threads into 2 even groups.

Step: 49: Take the left group and bundle them together, then on the left wing take the first thread at the top and tie a half hitch knot around the bundle, continue this till you have used each thread to tie a half hitch knot once.

Step 50: Repeat the process above on the right side of the owl; this should result in a piece that looks similar to the image below.

Step 51: Take four threads from both sides of the wings, as shown in the right picture below, and wrap them around the pole stick, shaping the owl's feet (left picture below).

Step 52: Take the threads from the edges and tie four square knots around the rest of the threads to secure the sitting pole firmly (see the two images below).

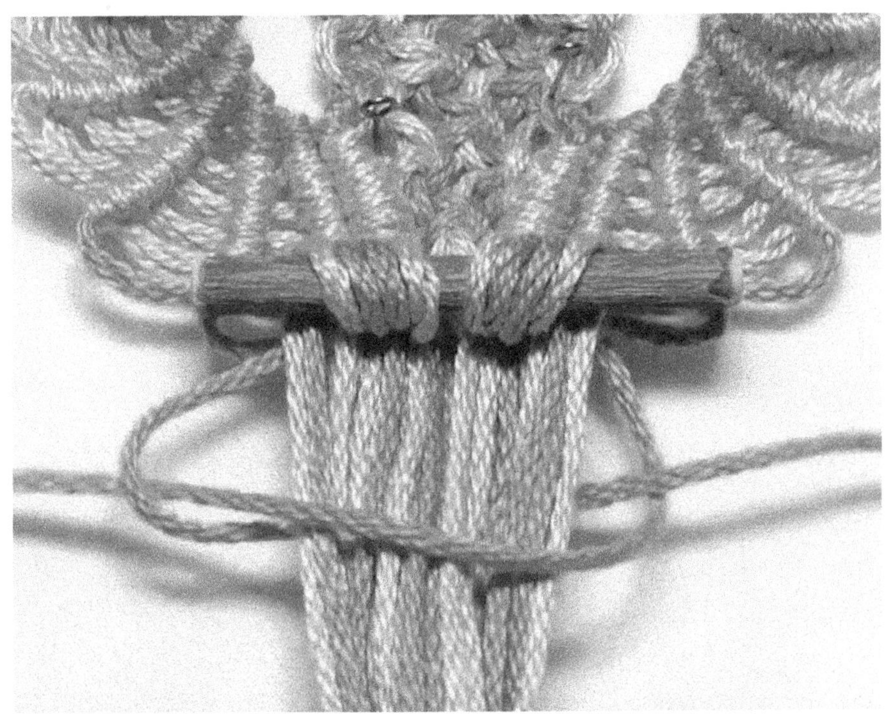

Step 53: Tie the strong knot behind your owl and cut the excessive edges.

And you're done!

Macramé Watch Strand

If you are looking for ways to spice up your wristwatch, well, now's

your chance! Make use of this Macramé Watch Strand Pattern and you will get what you want!

What you need:

Jump rings

Closure

2mm Crimp ends (you can choose another size, depending on your preferences)

Embroidery or craft floss

Watch with posts

Instructions:

Choose your types of floss, as well as their colors. Take at least 10 long

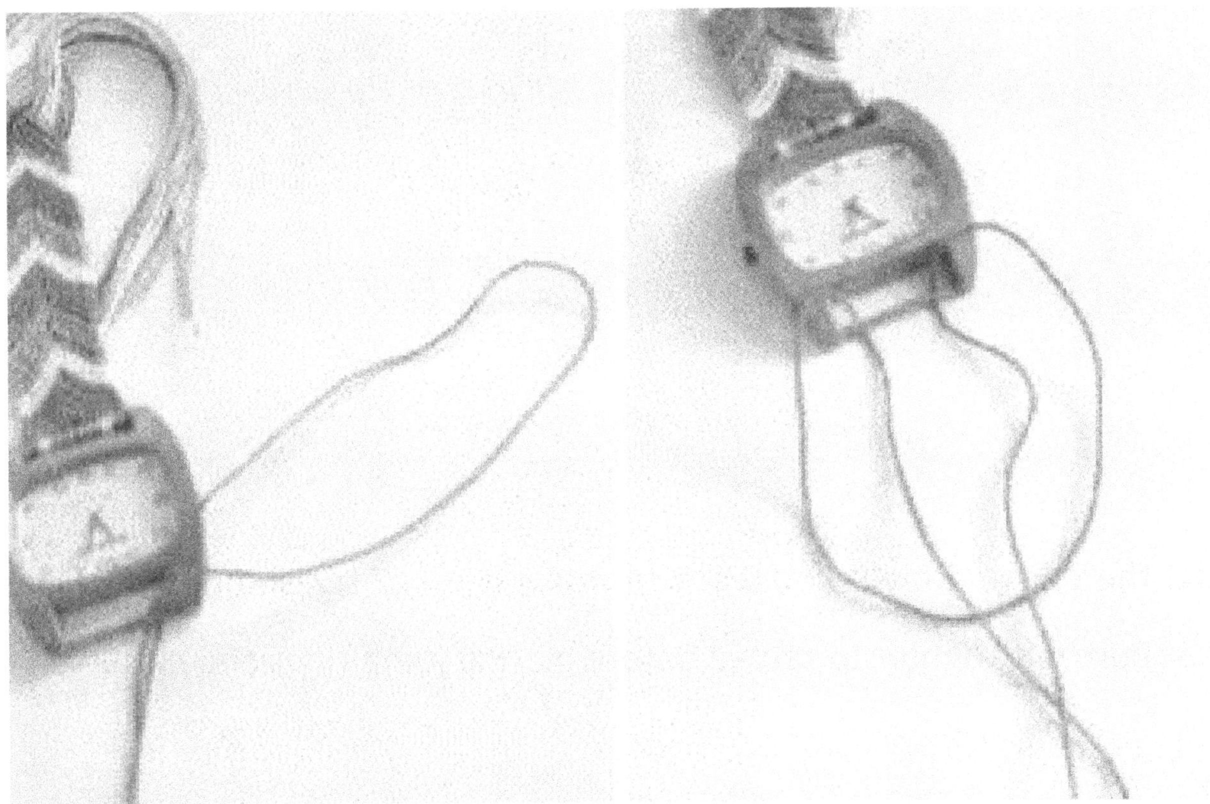

strands for each side of the watch.

Lash each floss onto the bar/posts of the watch and thread like you would a

regular Macramé bracelet or necklace.

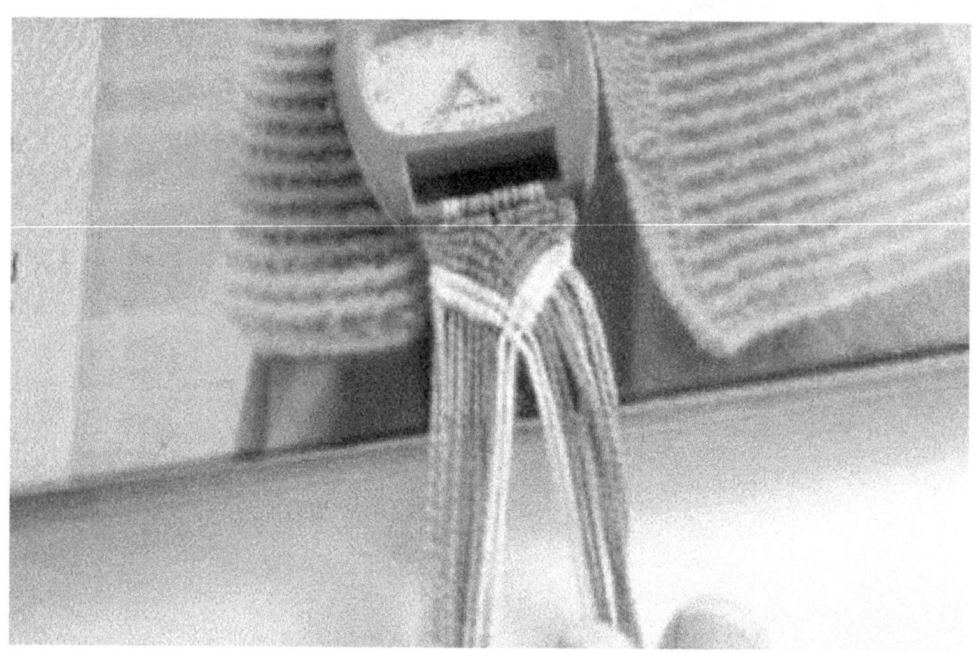

Braid the ends tightly if you want to make it more stylish and cut the ends. Burn with lighter to secure before placing jump rings and closure.

Use and enjoy!

Beginner's Bracelet

This is an easy Macramé project that's perfect for beginners!

What you need:

Glue-on end clasps

Jewelry glue

Ring connector

Cotton or hemp twine

Instructions:

First, take three of the hemp or cotton twine strands and make a loop out of them. Loop the loop that you have made around the connector

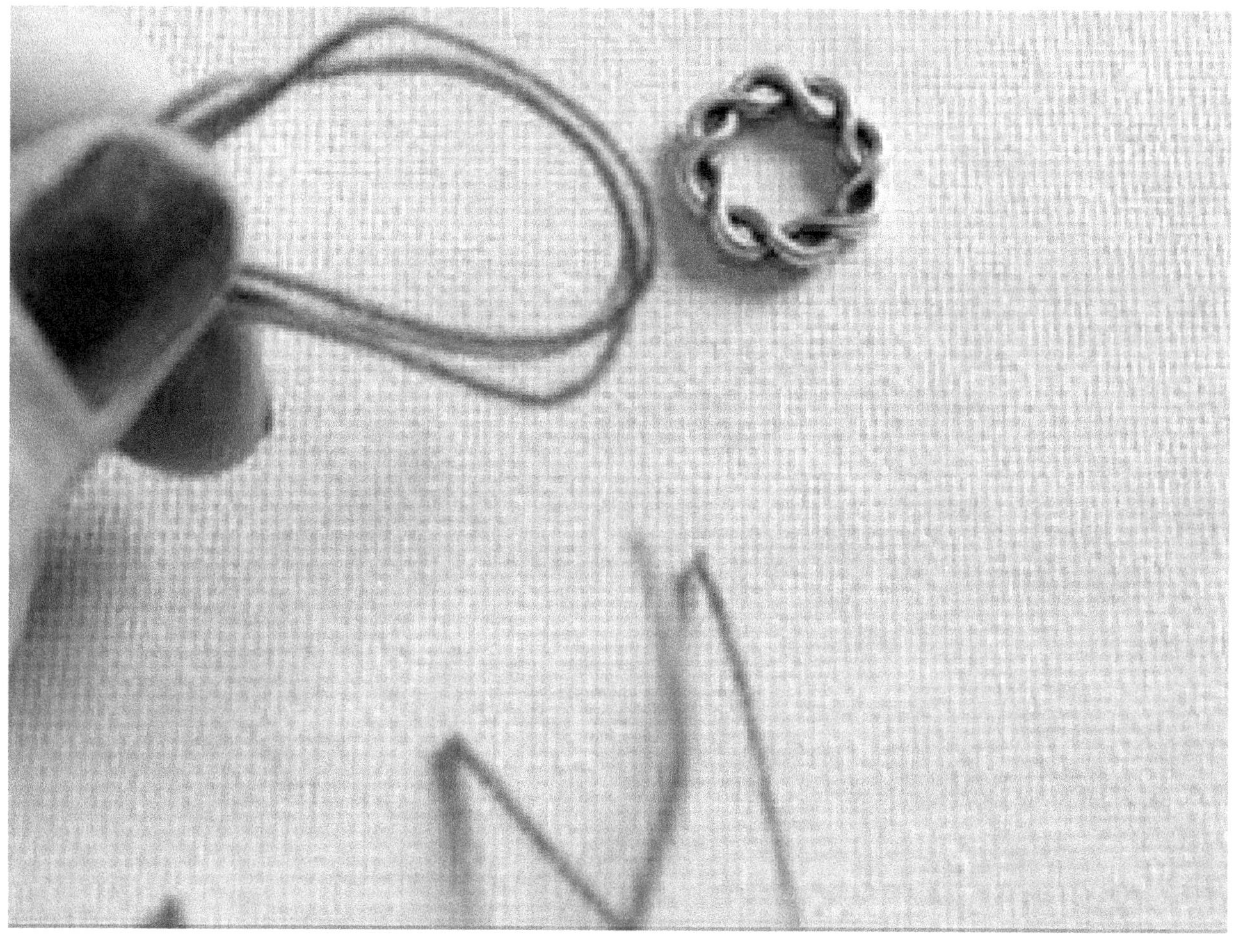

and then make a knot on each side.

Now, you'll see 6 strands coming off the sides of your loop after you have inserted it through the connector. Braid each side—you can make simple braids, or even 6-strand braids, if you can do it.

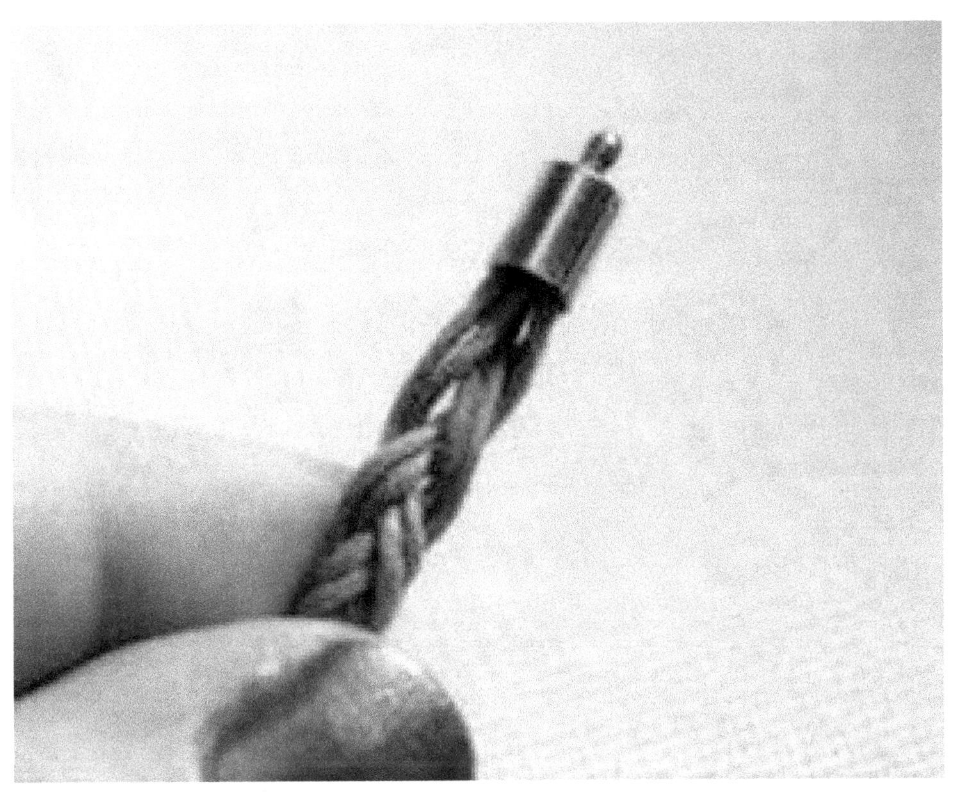

Trim the ends off once you get to the end. Make sure to use jewelry glue and secure the braid by gluing it on. Fully twist the end caps to coat the spine of your bracelet. Check the length before securing so you can be sure that it would really fit you.

Intricate Lavender Macramé

Lavender is a really nice color and seeing it on a Macramé bracelet is always good. This project is pretty dainty, and could really help you use your time well as it needs loads of focus!

What You Need:

Disposable Plastic Cup

Headpins

Scissors

Glue

26 pieces 4mm crystal bicones

28 pieces size 6 Color A seeds

26 pieces size 11 seeds

4 pieces rectangular 6 x 4 mm glass bugles

2 pieces size 6 Color B seeds

1 open ended circular memory wire

C-Lon Nylon cord, divided into two: 5 ½ ft. long working cord, and 1 ft. long centerpiece cord

Instructions:

Use the disposable plastic cup to anchor the memory wire in. This way, you could prevent it from falling down as you work on your project.

Pass the middle of the working cord under the wire. Go ahead and wrap a square knot around it. Now, make sure that your two cords are already of the same length.

Then, string one of the size 6 seeds on each cord before making 2 more square knots and tying the bicord the way you tied the 6 seeds. Make sure that the knots are going in one direction and that they have uniformity.

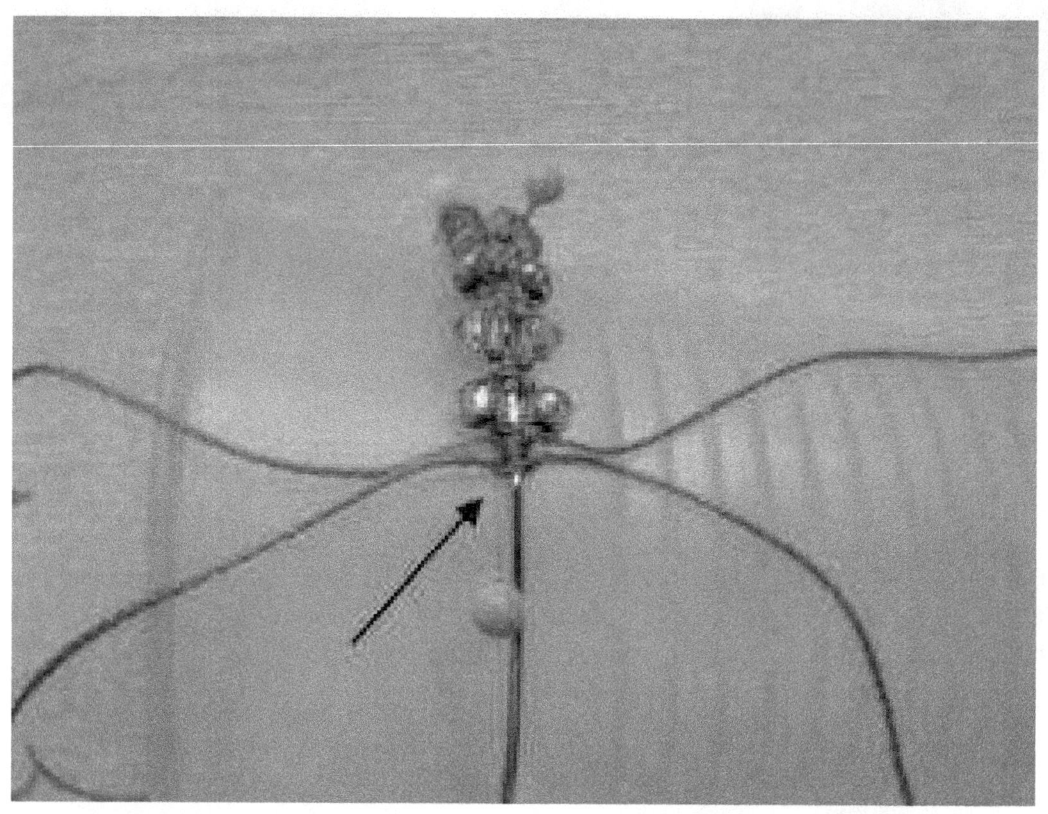

Work enough portions until you reach the middle then add the final two beads with one square knot.

The new cord will now be your anchor so make sure that you tie it around the original cord. Repeat on the other side.

Repeat until you reach the end of the wire so you could knot 2 square knots. Slide the end cords in with tapestry needle and then cut and glue the shortest way you can, just to keep it secure, and aesthetically good, of course. Cut the excess cords and finally tie with an overhand knot.

Rhinestone Macramé Bracelet

This bracelet is really colorful, easy on the eyes, and is quite customizable—so it's up to you if you want to add more beads, use more colors, and the like.

What you need:

Lighter

Scissors

Tape

Embroidery needle

1 small rhinestone button

1 large rhinestone button

3 yards 0.8mm Chinese knitting cord

Instructions:

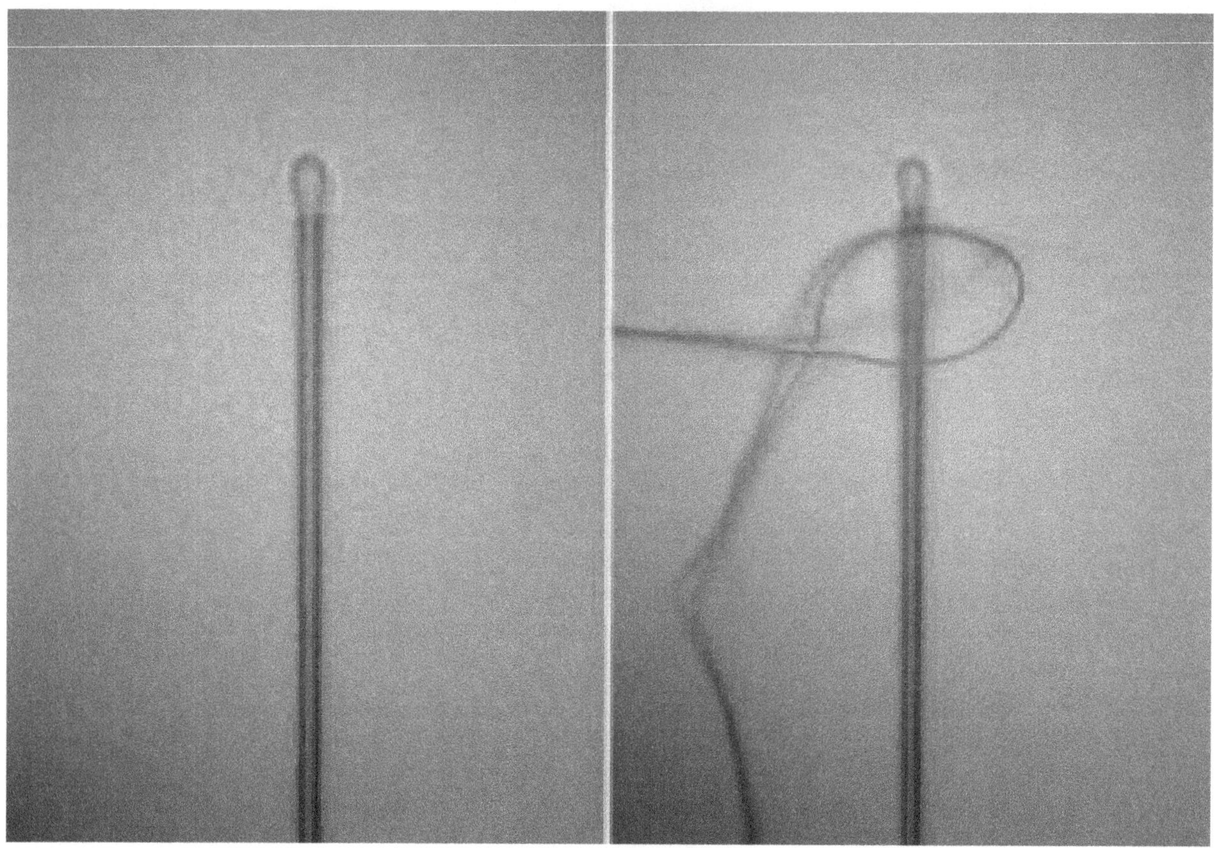

Cut knotting cord into 80" and 20" pieces.

Then, fold the smaller cord in half and find the center of the long cord. Make sure the center of the cord is under the two strands in the middle, and make sure it goes under the left cord.

Next, pull the cord on the left all the way to the right and middle straps

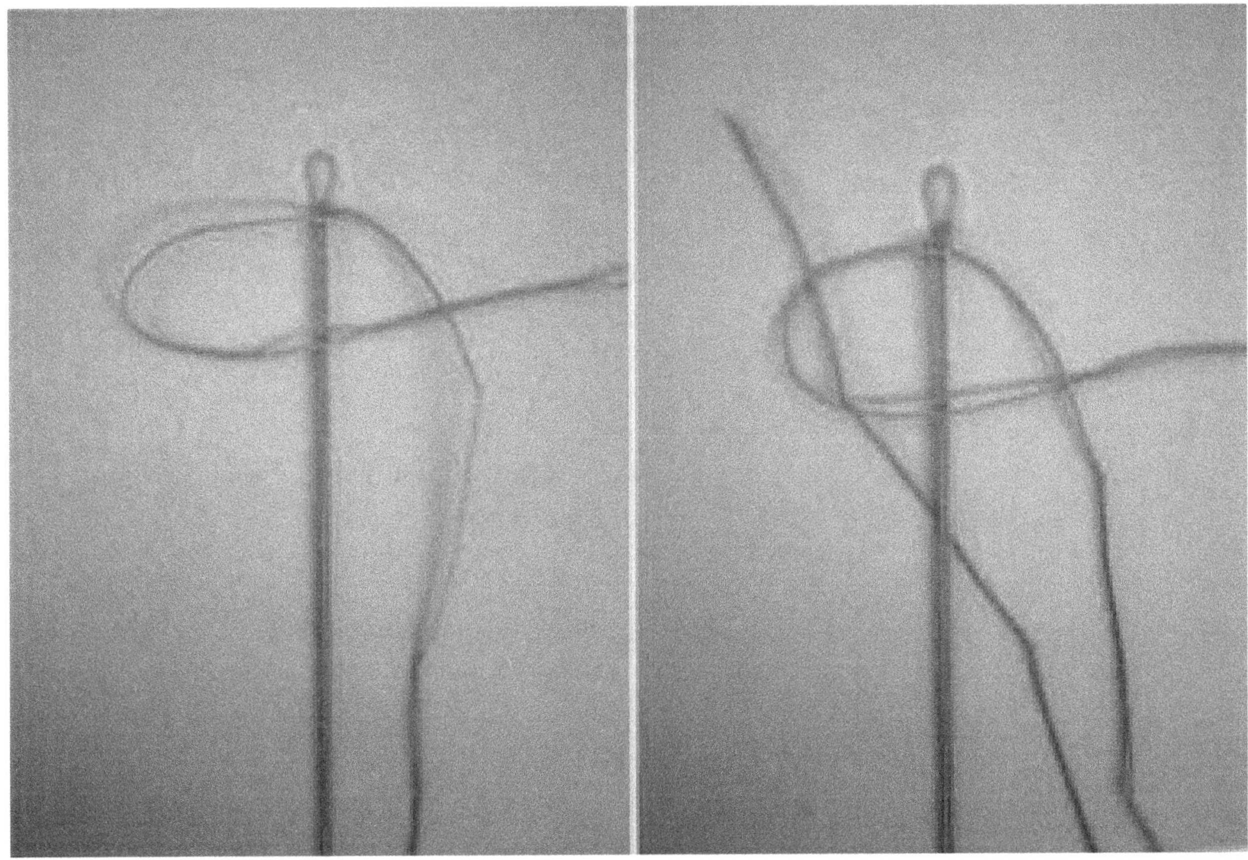

so that the loop could go through to the right side. Slide the loop over the right rhinestone button.

Make continuous square knots on the left side. Repeat the steps after pulling

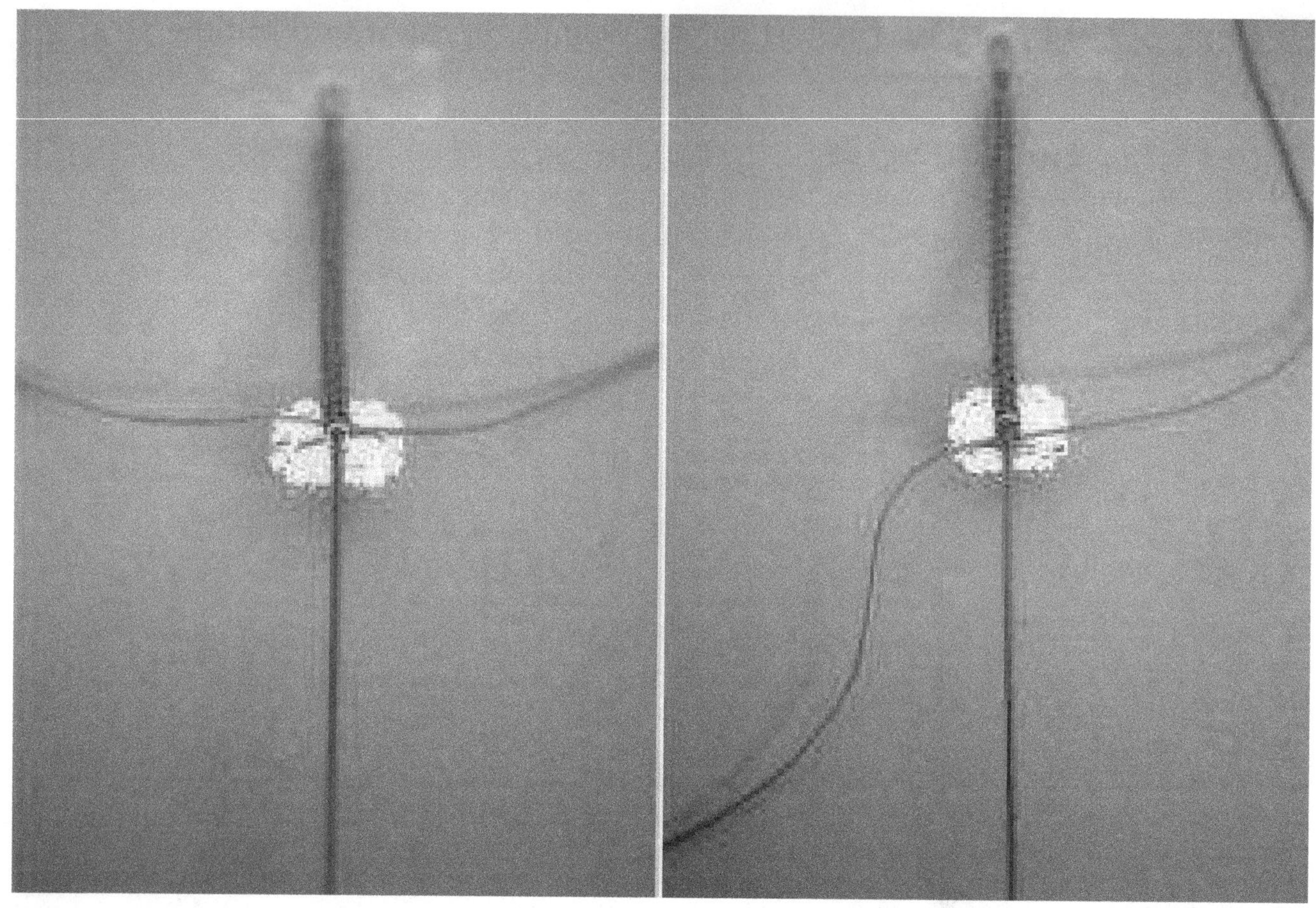

tightly and stop knotting when you reach your desired length.

Now, get the large rhinestone button and thread it onto the 2 strands in the middle. Knot some more and add the small rhinestone button near the end, just before you close the loop.

Enjoy your new Macramé bracelet!

Stand Spiral Bracelet

This one has quite a lot of layers to it—but it's really beautiful and is something you could give away as a friendship bracelet. Now, you won't have problems looking for gifts to give away to your friends anymore!

What you need:

- Scissors
- Rattail cords (interior/exterior colors)
- Kumihino round disk
- ruler

Instructions:

Get 4 cuttings of your interior colors, and 4 cuttings of the outer color. It's up to you what colors you want to use—just make sure they complement each other. Cut the exterior color to be 45 inches long,

and the interior one to be 39 inches long. Find the center of the cords as you hold them together.

Find the front of the round disk and place the center of the cords there.

Lace the disk like you see on the image below.

Now, take the bottom left cord and cross it above the top left cord.

Take the bottom right cord and cross it above the top right cord.

Take the upper left cord and cross it above the bottom left cord.

Take the upper right cord and cross it above the bottom right cord.

Turn the disk, and repeat the process on the cords on the other side of

the disk. You'll then notice the cords coming out of the backside.

When you feel like the length and the look of the bracelet are alright with you, go ahead and take all the cords and pinch them so they wouldn't come undone.

Take the bracelet off the disk and knot the end to close. Secure with glue and let dry before using.

Studded Macramé Bracelet

This studded bracelet is sure to up your accessory game. It's simple but not bland. It's also regal, but definitely not overwhelming.

What you need:

Two binder clips

Bent nose pliers

Needle

Nipper tool

Clipboard

GS Hypo Cement

Two 6mm/ 1.8 mm hole multi-cut rounds

30 4mm Sterling Silver multi-cut rounds

1 Swarovski Trapeze button

3 yards neutral leather cord

1 yard natural leather cord

Instructions:

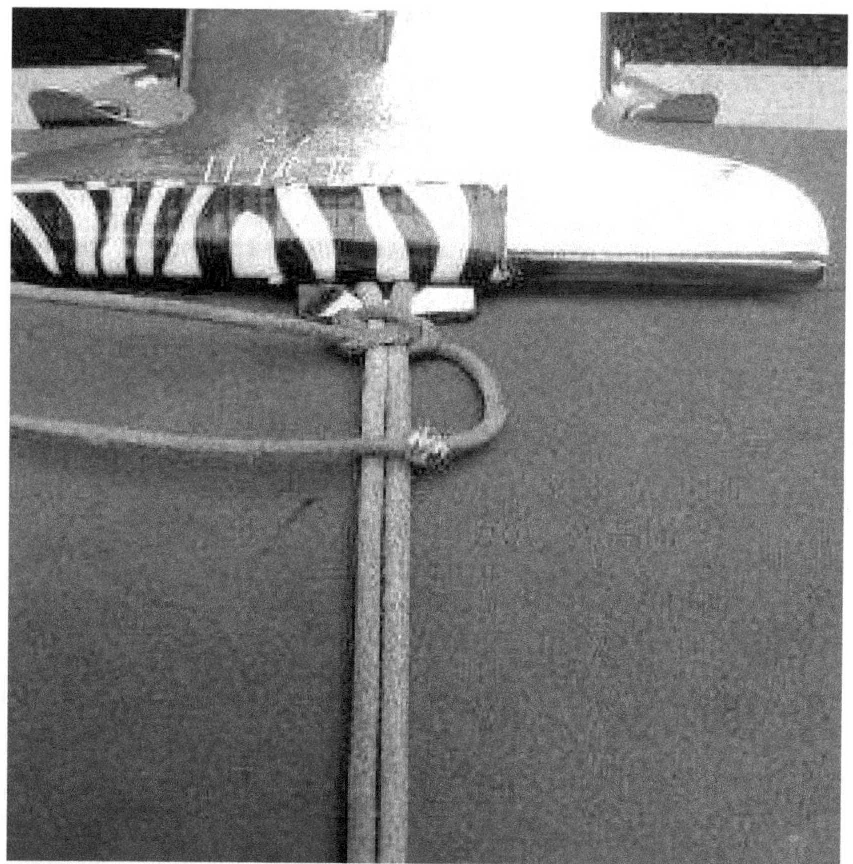

Nip the ends of the leather cord so you could insert the 4mm beads.

Then, take the leather cord and slide it down the button. Make sure to center the button on the clipboard.

Center the leather cord on your 2mm cords, and then take the knotting cord over the left cord. Take the left part under the center and loop up to the right side. Take the right cord over the left side. Make sure to pull the cords tightly, and then let the right knotting cord pass under the center cord through the side loop. Make

sure to tightly pull both of the cords together.

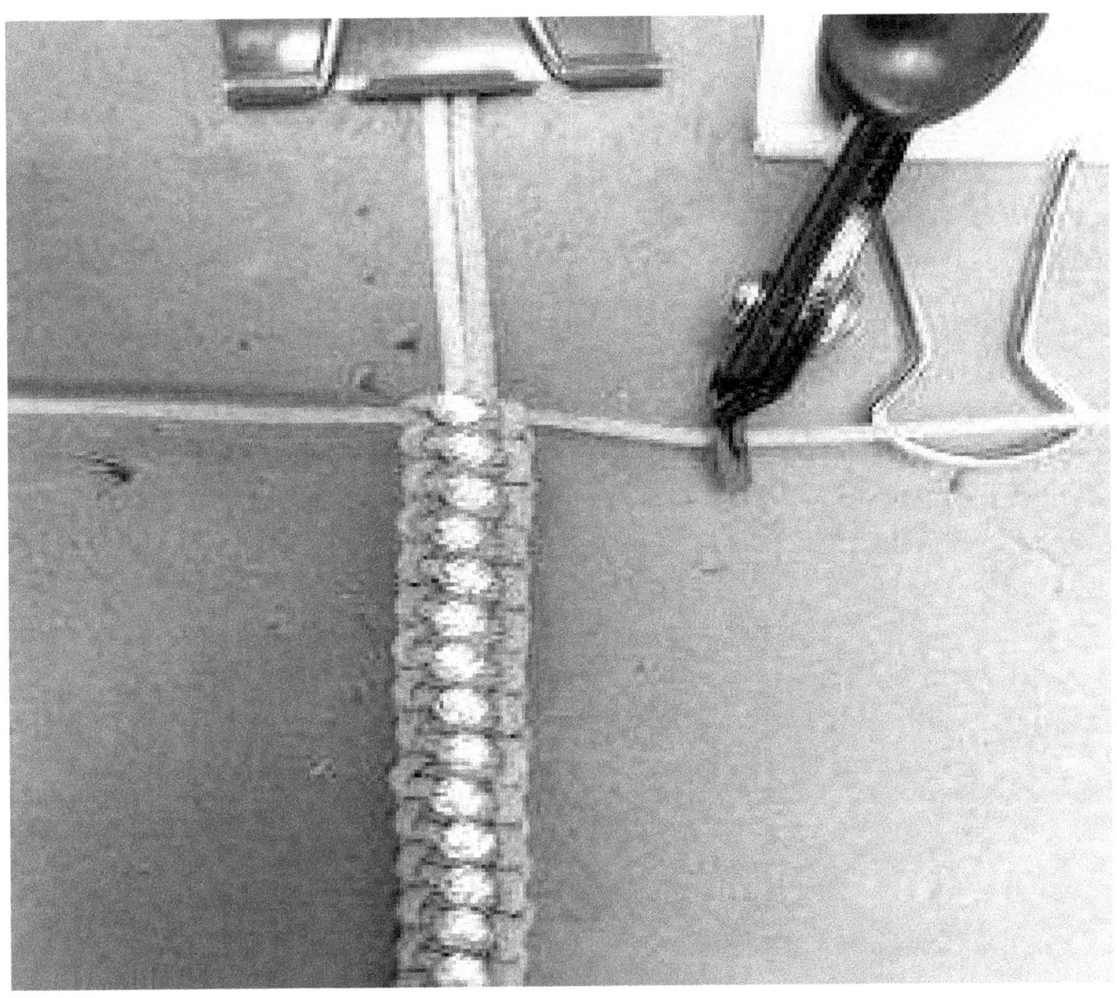

Repeat until you have used all of your thread, and then start adding the multi-cut beads until you reach your desired length.

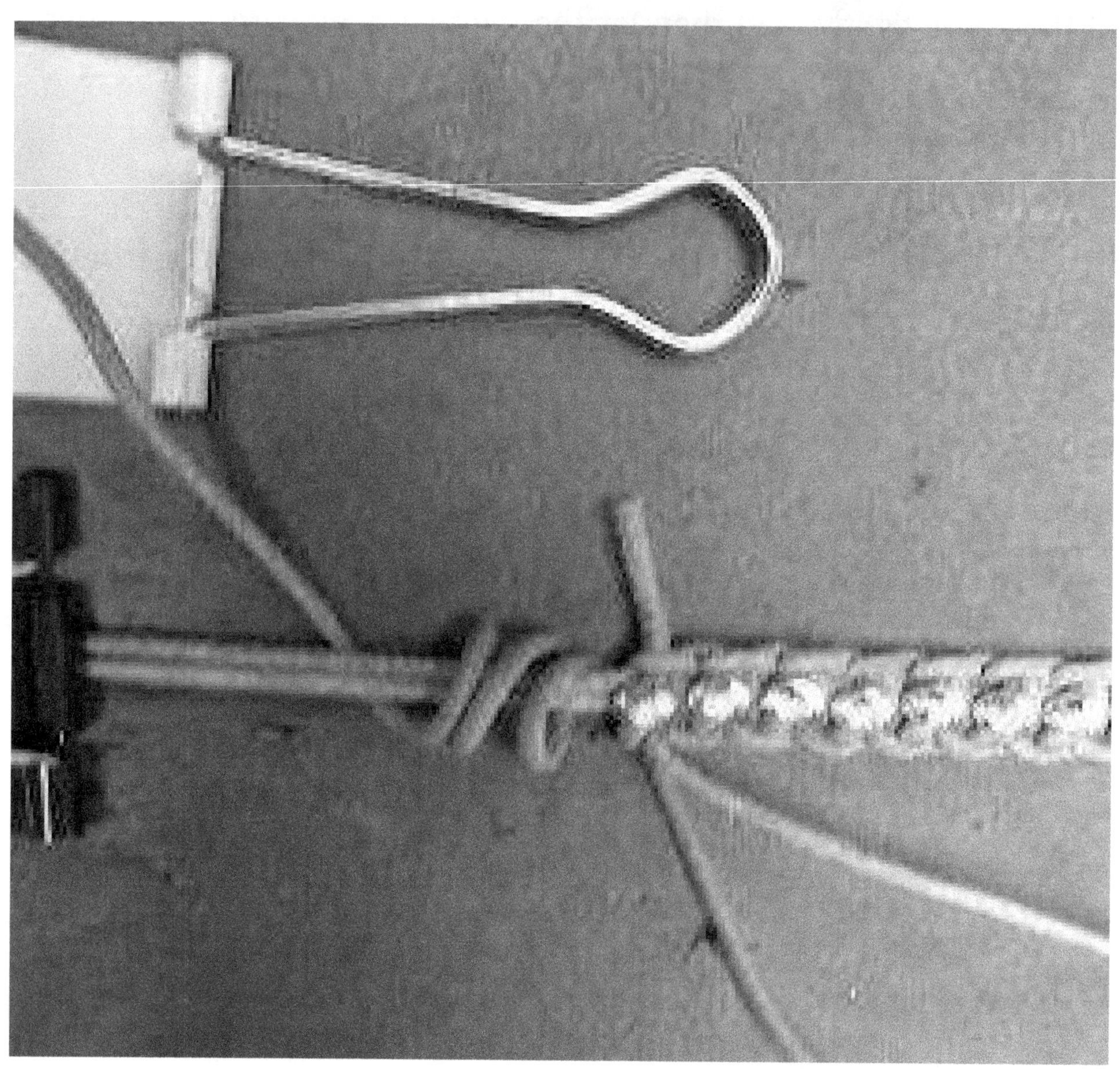

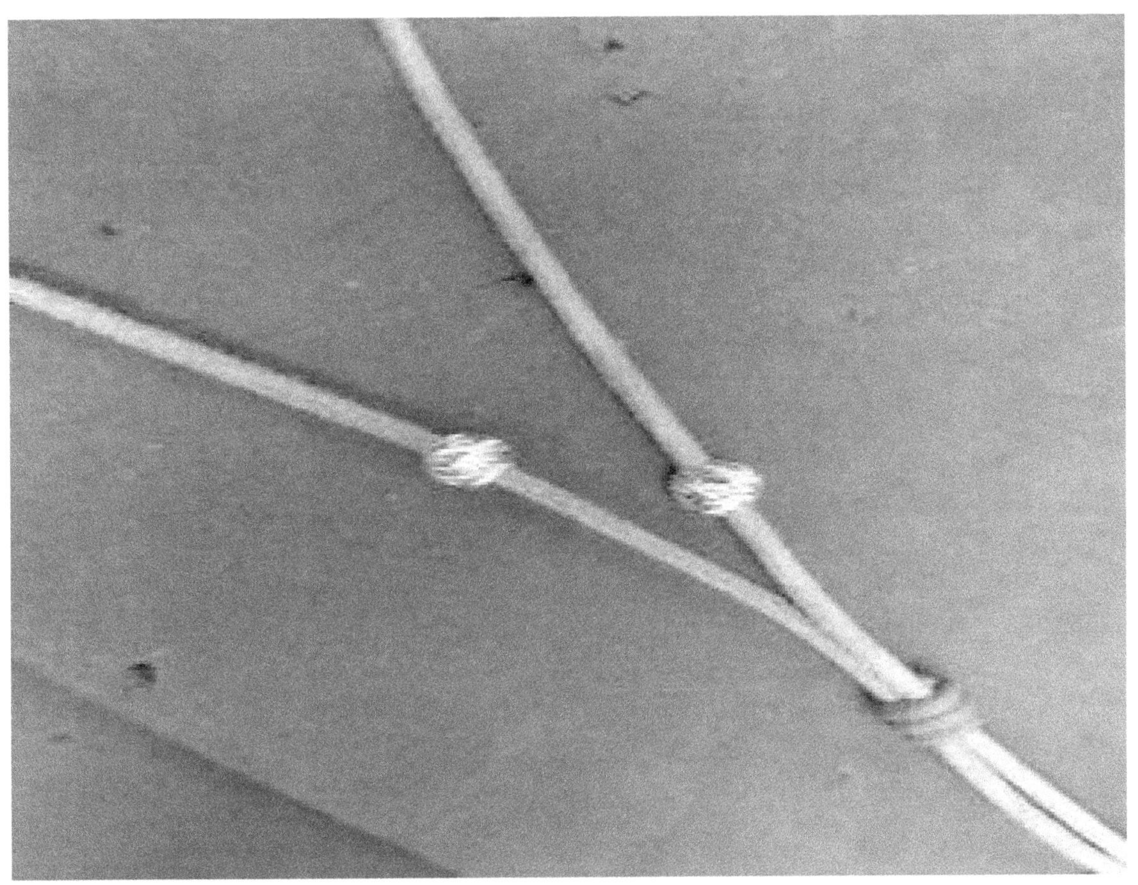

Clip the excess cord and leave just around ¾ of it. Make sure to center

some on the cord and to wrap at least 2 mm around the cord. Slide at least three loops up, and then take the excess cord and thread it around the three loops.

To make the button hole, just make sure to pull the cord roughly until you get 1.5mm of knotting cord in your hands.

Add the Sterling multi-cut beads on the end of the leather cords and make a knot to let the embellishment sit.

Seal with hypo cement (don't worry, it's nothing like cement used for constructing houses), let dry, and use!

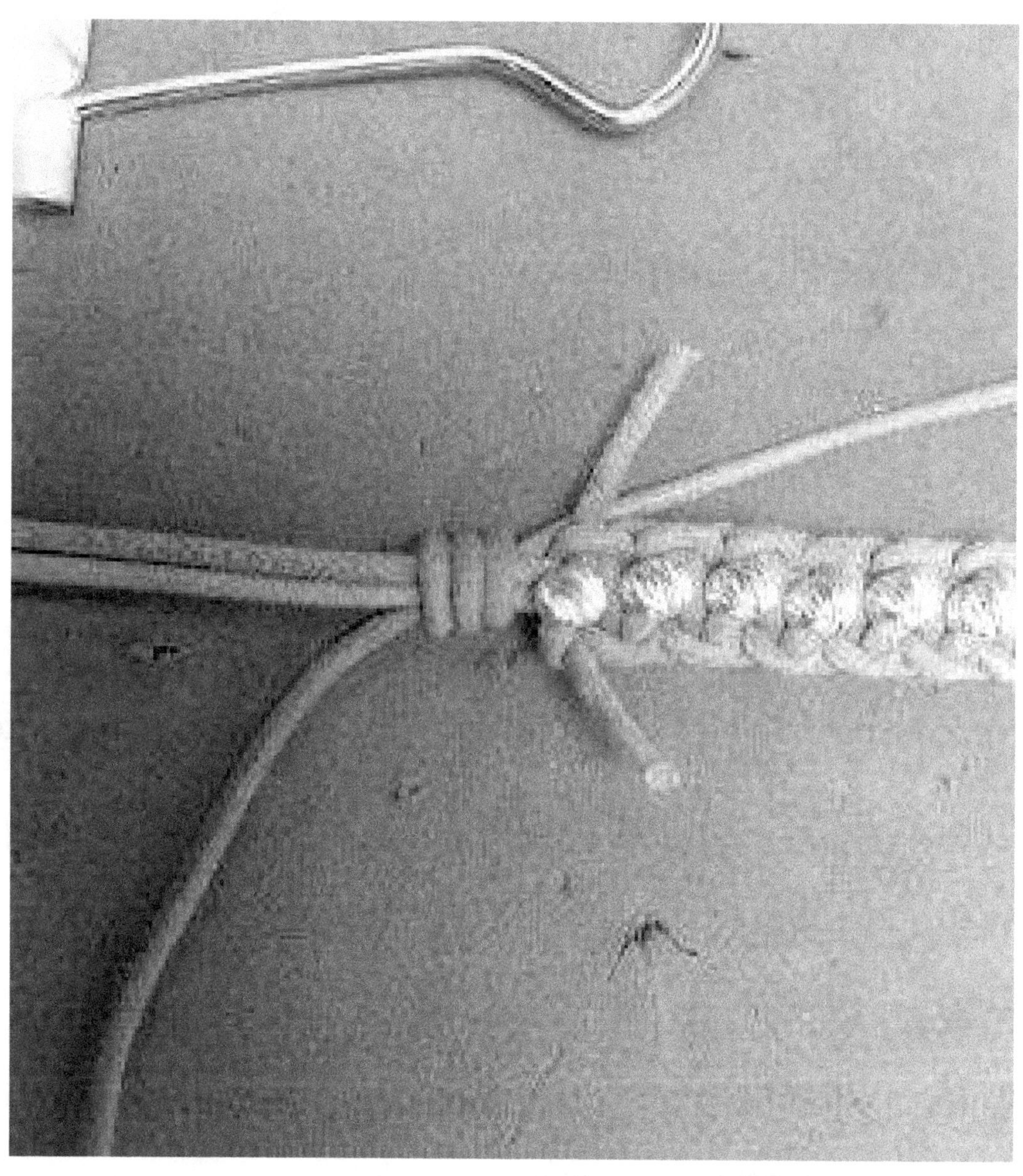

Dip-Dyed Macramé DIY Elegant Necklace

On one side, include all three ends caps to a 12mm dive ring.

Like many crafting methods, it makes more sense the more you do it.

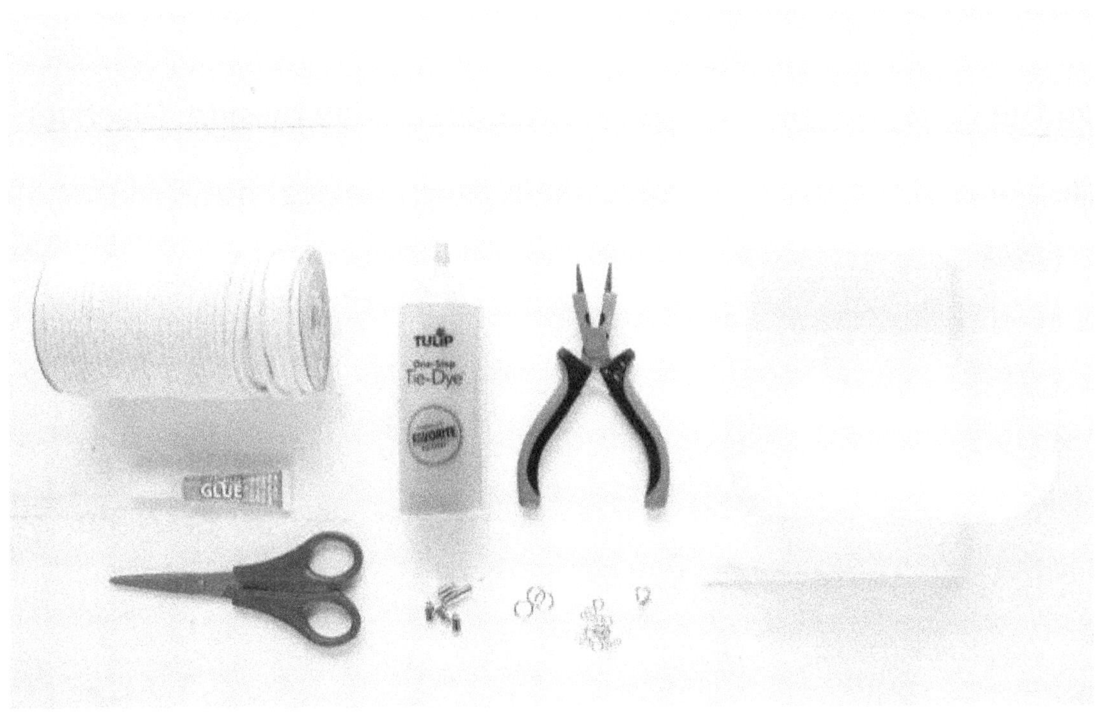

With some practice, you'll be able to produce a flexible, attractive macramé DIY device.

1. Cut three hairs of macramé rope, determining at least 36 inches each.

2. Position the hairs of rope on a flat surface area, side by side. Discover the middle point of the rope trio and take a psychological note

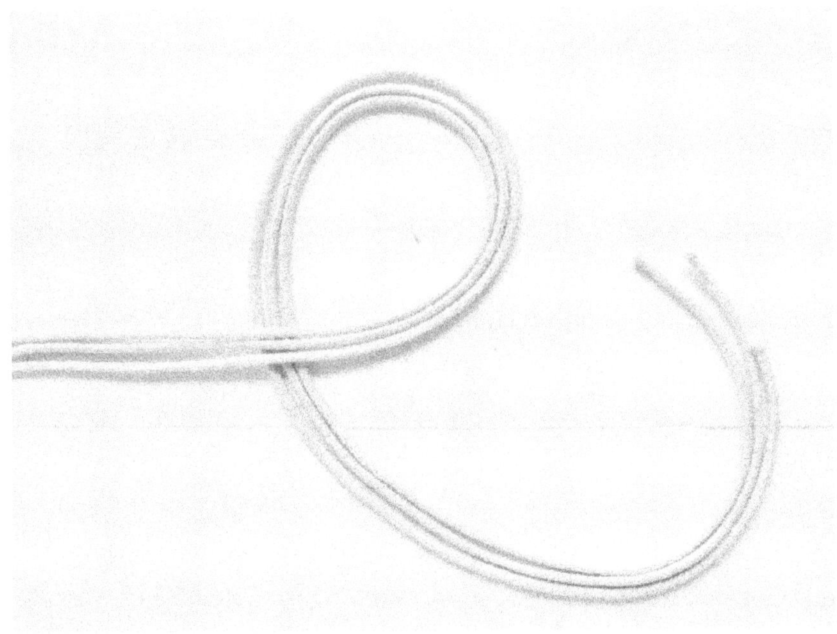

3. Take the best end of the rope and location it below itself.

4. Bring completion of the rope up.

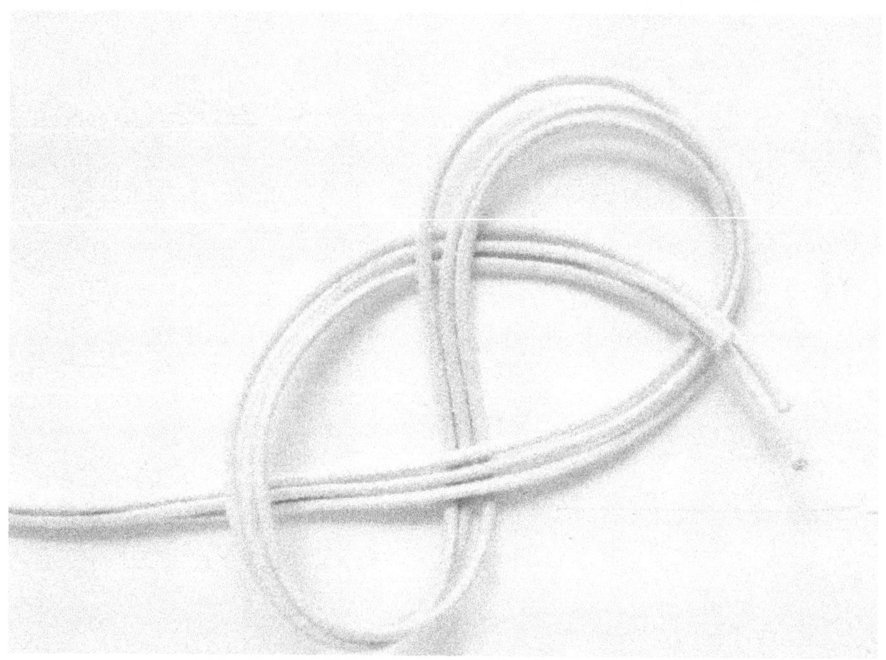

5. Location completion beneath the loop and directly through.

6. Pull carefully. This develops a single completed knot.

7. Now, it's time to deal with the left side. Bring the other end over the rope, positioning it near the knot your simply produced.

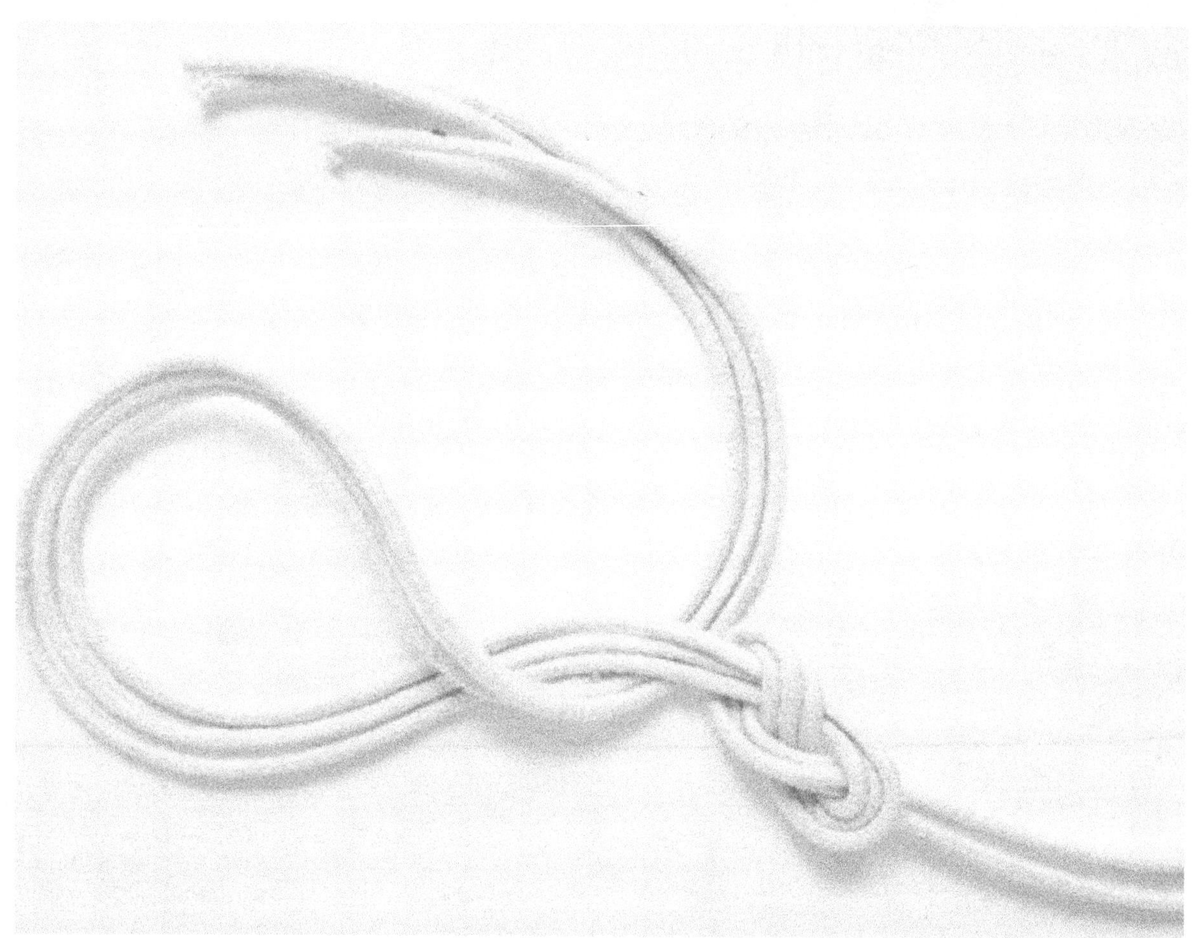

8. Bring completion beneath the rope and up. At this point, a loop will form

9. Place completion through the loop, positioning it over then under and directly through.

10. Pull carefully to finish the 2nd knot. Reverse the knot and re-position till you have actually attained your wanted appearance if required.

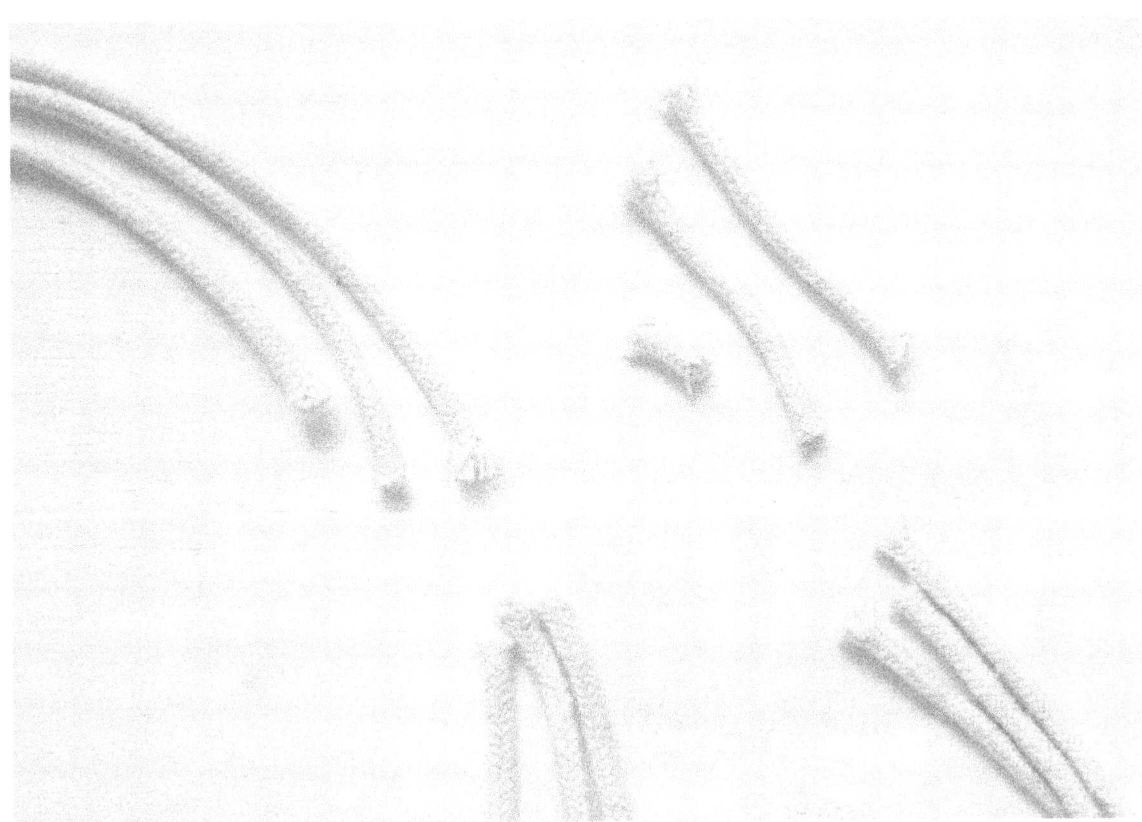

11. Trim completions of the rope.

You can dip color the knots or the whole piece. It's completely as much as you!

12. Location of the macramé DIY cable inside the container.

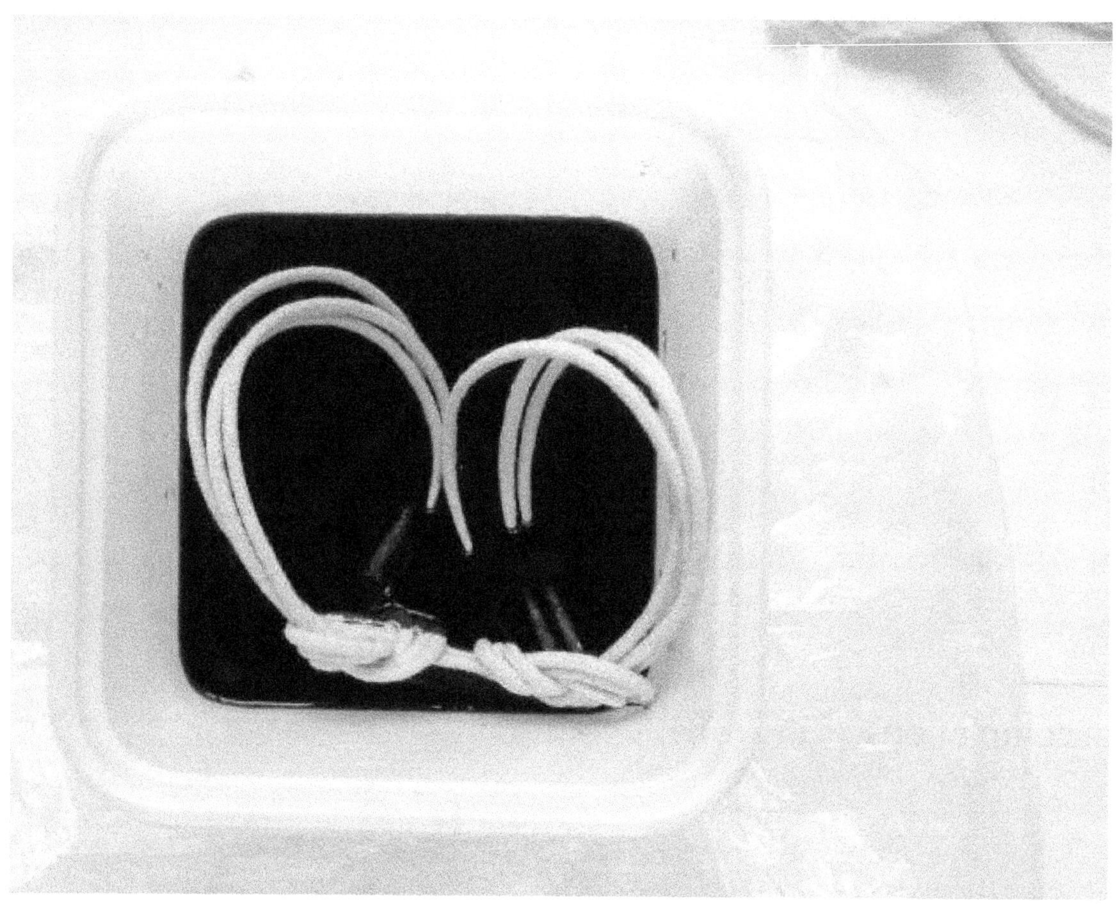

13. Under running water, wash the rope till the water turns clear. Set out to dry entirely

14. Optional: For additional information, including three 7mm dive rings to each hair of rope. Utilize the flattening part of the pliers to protect each dive ring

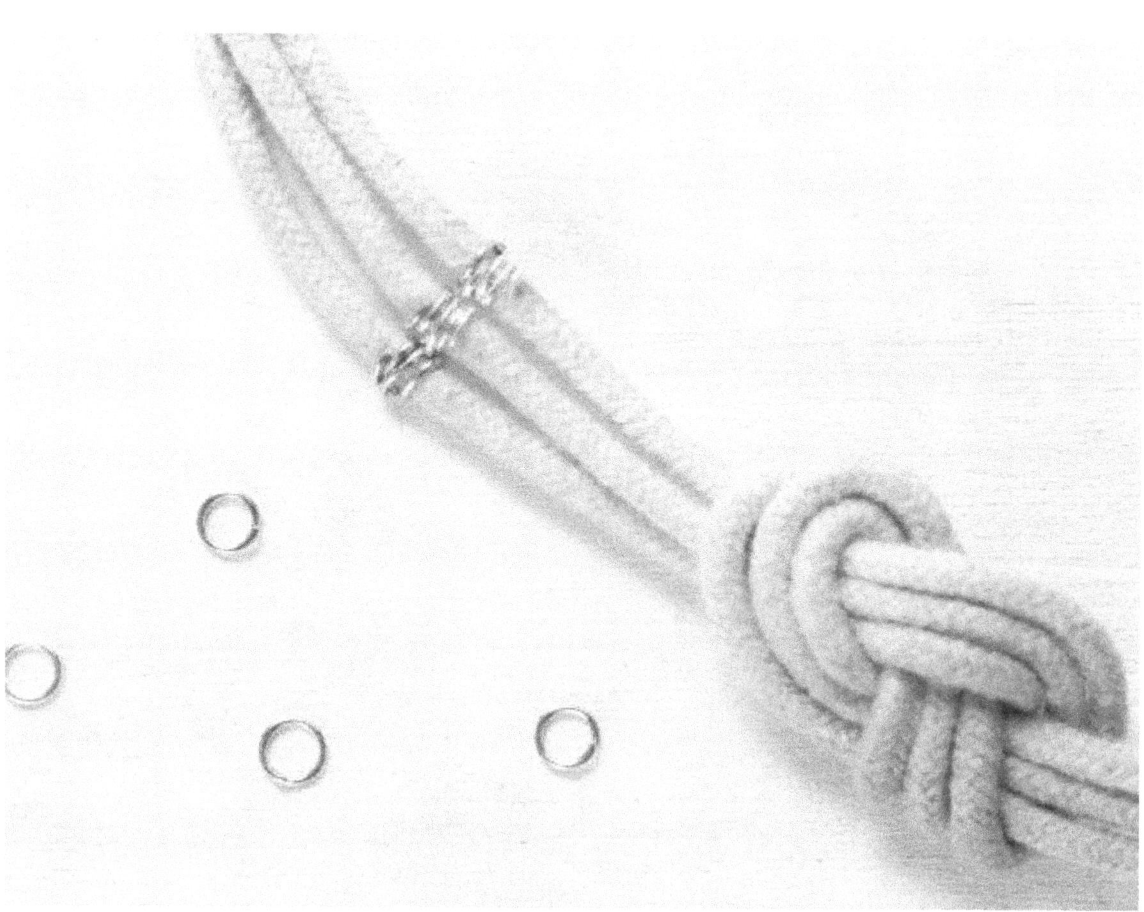

15. Glue 5mm end caps to the ends of the rope. Delegate dry

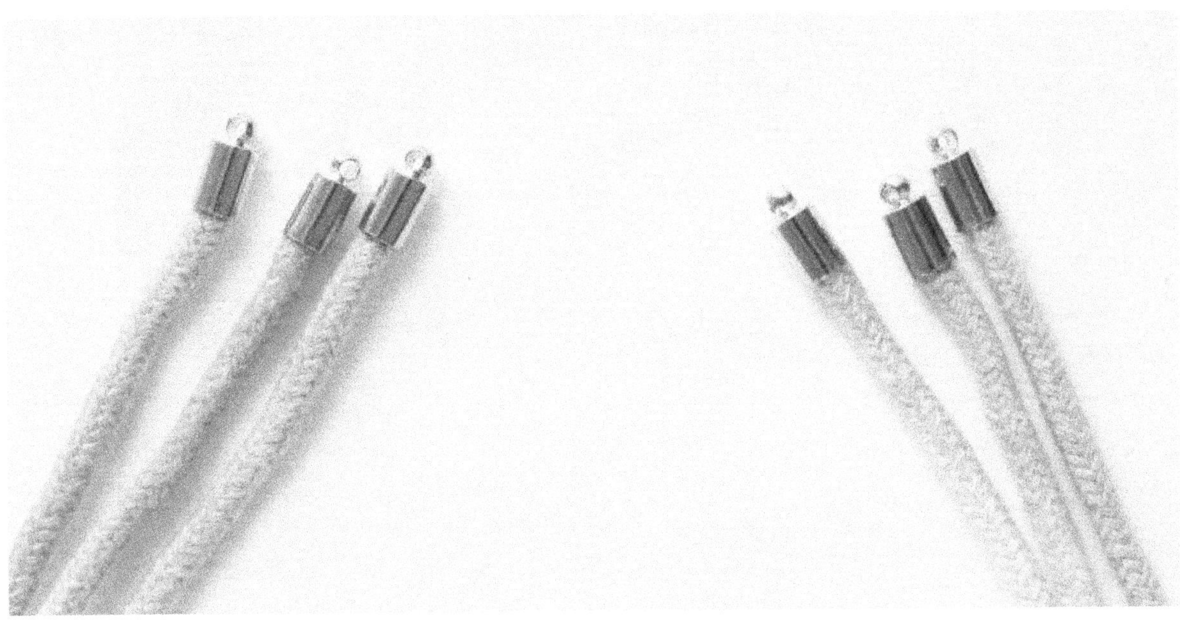

Take the macrame pattern. Fortunately, you do not require to be a macrame pro to take on this dip-dyed macrame DIY pendant. With a couple of creative knots and standard natural macrame cables, you can accept the pattern in your own closet.

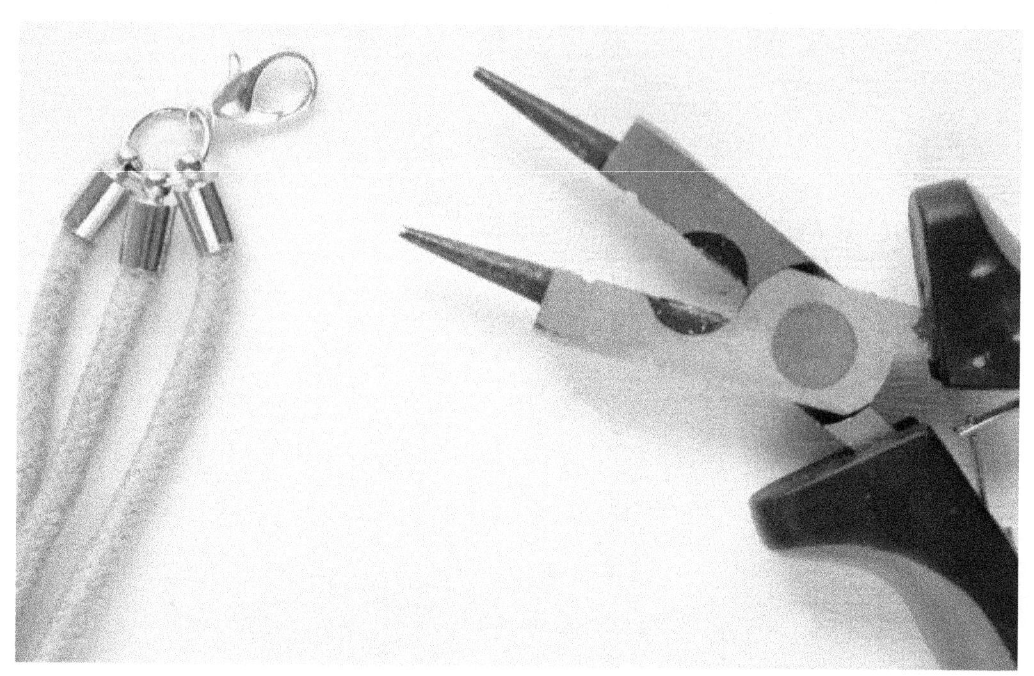

Knotted Chevron Headband

Supplies:

– Broder floss (6 colors/12 suits my 1/2-inch wide headband)

– The satin narrow belt – 1/8 to 1/4 "is perfect.

– E6000 or equivalent adhesive plastic

– 1/2 centimeter long or your favorite headband

– Matched thread and needle sewing

– preferably if you want to place the knotted portion on the headband for extra stability

Instructions

Start by making your extra-long friendship bracelet.

I've been using 6 strands each 10 feet in length, half by 5 feet, but if your head band is wider, maybe your headband would be bigger.

Hold a removable knot together and tie the strands and operate the Classic Chevron Friendship Bracelet (or pattern for you) until the strip is 1 to 5 inches longer than the length of the headband.

Untie the knot upon completion.

Put a dot of glue on the back of your headband and put it around your headband. Make sure you cover the band on the front and back and if you have a single face on the satin belt, the good side is off.

Cut off the tails one end of the knitted strip and hold it down. Save it for a few minutes.

Put some glue on your back and tie the knotted strip to the rope until it is imperfect.

So go on gluing and binding, but then behind the knotted thread.

Avoid gluing and wrapping when the knotted strip is as far away from the other end.

Cut the tails to the end and add the whole length of the super long bracelet to the end. Likely, you will extend it a little to match and that's perfect. (Keep it to the end only if you want to stitch the kneaded portion on the back).

Hold on the end of the strip and tie it smoothly on your back to the end of the headband.

When you just hang up, you can thread the knotted piece back and forth on the edges and draw it close. This is a good

Silky Purple Necklace

This silky necklace looks quite regal as it is in the color of purple. With the help of rhinestones, it becomes all the more elegant!

What you need:

Rhinestones

Clasp

2 inches of chain

Thread and needle (in the same color scheme)

6 yards silk rattail cord

Instructions:

Cut string into 6 yards, and the other to be 36 inches. Make sure that you loop the last chain link.

Make use of square knots to tie the outer cord with the inner cord, and make sure to overlap on the left. Bring the string's end right under the center strings. Knot by pulling the right and left ends of the cord.

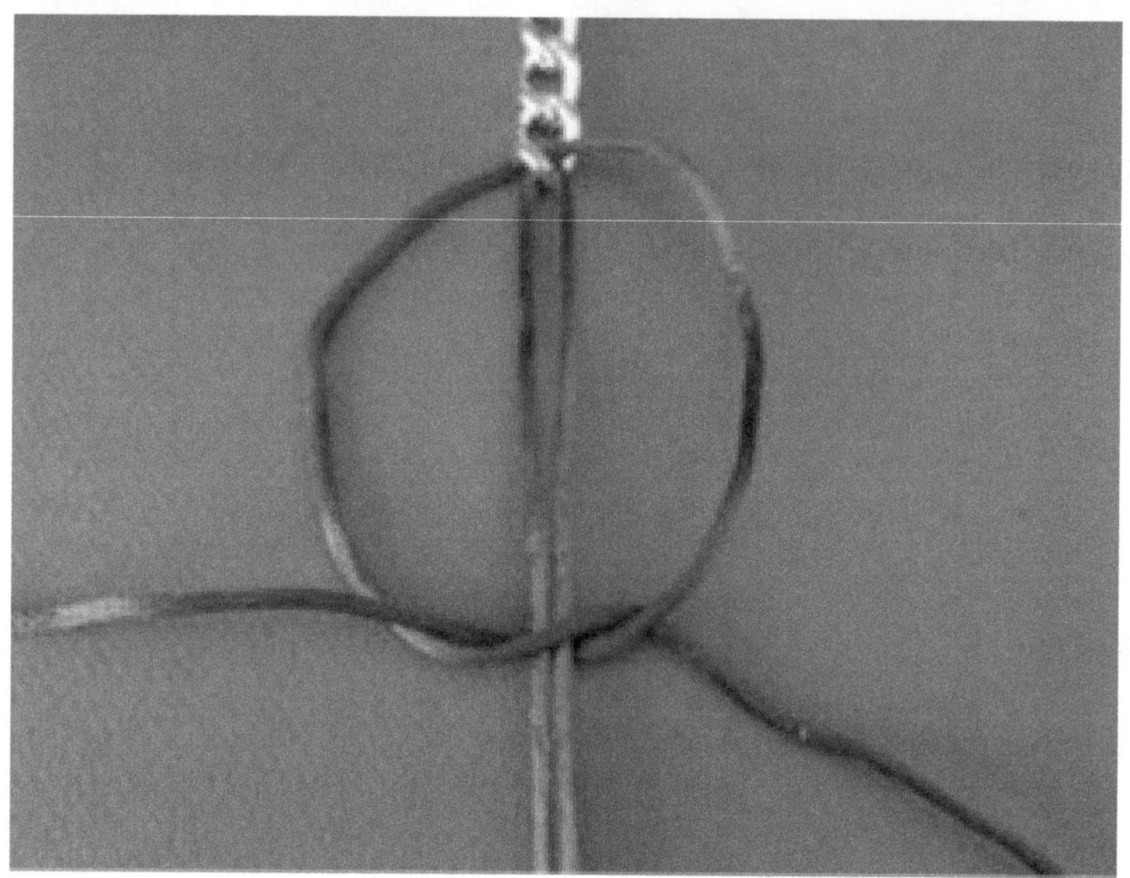

Repeat the process on the opposite side of the chain and make sure to pull tight through the loop and make use of square knots until you reach your desired length.

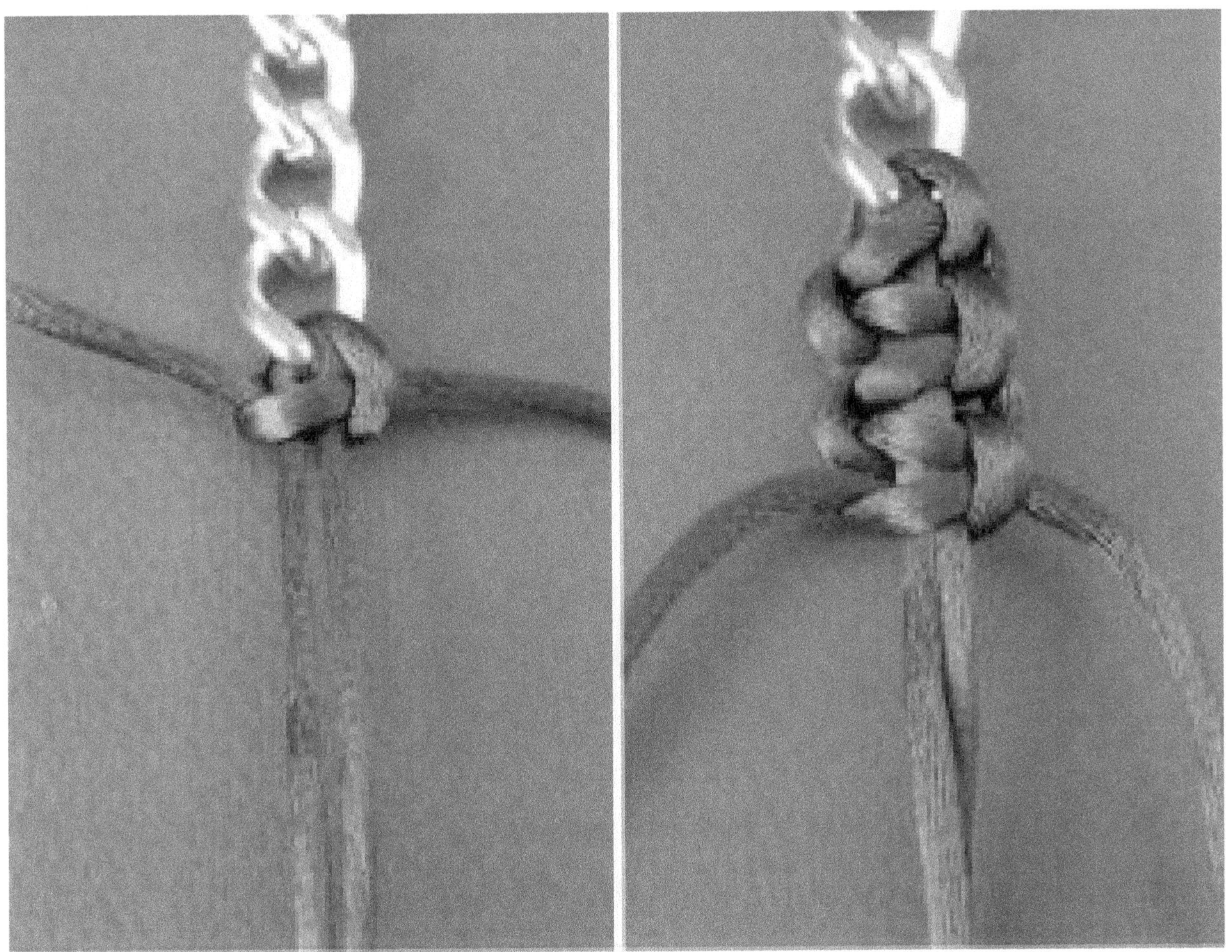

Double knot the cord once you read your desired length so you could lock it up. Make use of fabric glue to secure the ends of the cord together.

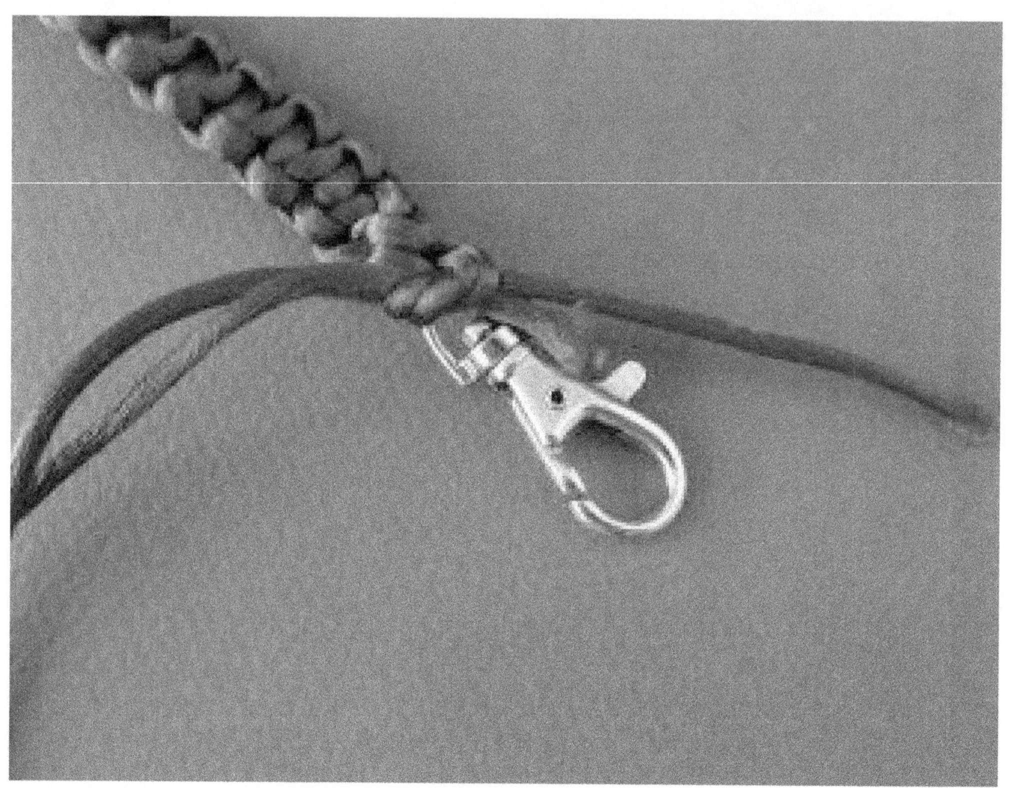

Attach rhinestones with glue and let dry before using.

Enjoy your new necklace!

Leathery Knotted Necklace

A leather necklace has that rustic and earthy feel. Now, if you want to add some edge to an already beautiful thing, you could try Macramé and go and knot the thread!

What you need:

Pliers

Scissors

Chain

Crimp ends

Jump rings

Clasp

7 silver beads

5 meters of leather cord

Instructions:

Cut leather into a meter each and make 4 parts, then make a four-strand braid out of it.

Make use of the square knot to secure the loops. Copy on the left side of the cord.

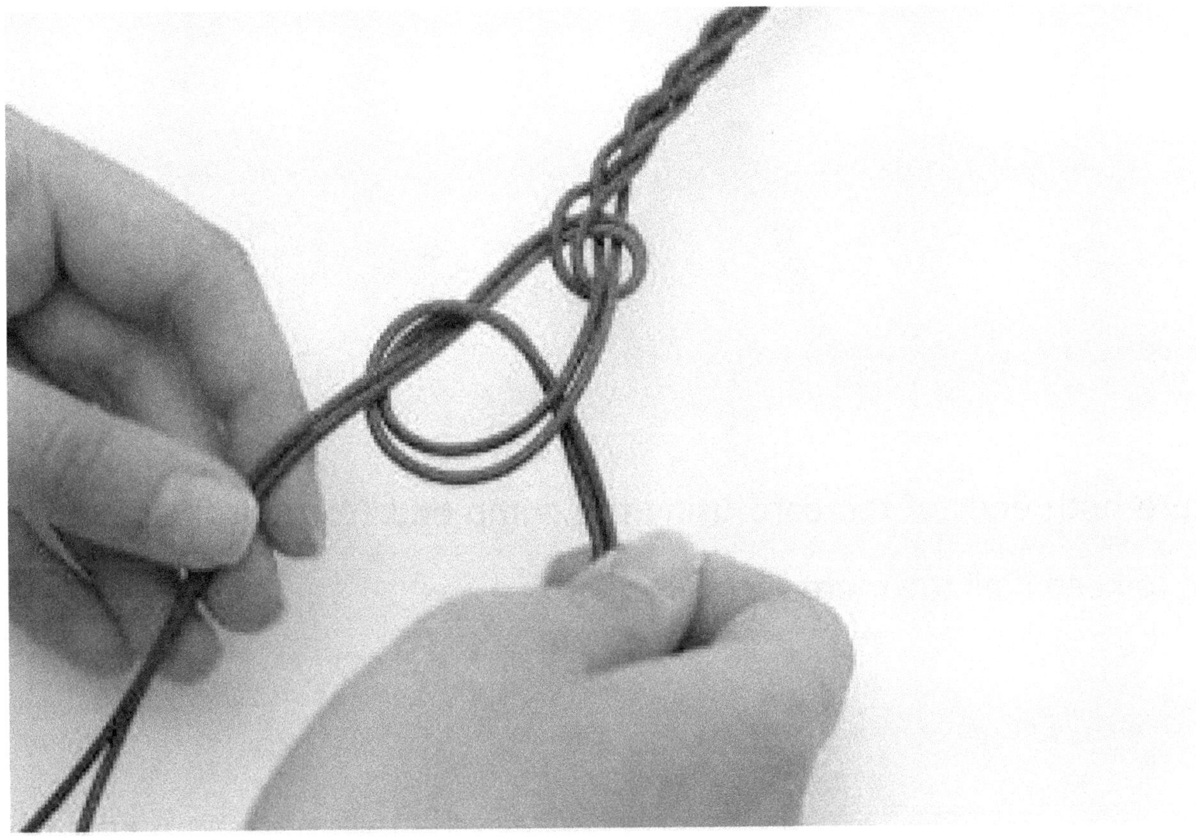

Add beads after you have done the first two knots. Hold it as you hold the right string. Create an empty knot, loop, and add some beads again.

Secure both ends of the cord using the crimp end. You could also use glue to keep it all the more secure.

Attach a piece of the chain at the end with a jump ring so your necklace could be ready.

Enjoy your new necklace!

Macramé Gem Necklace

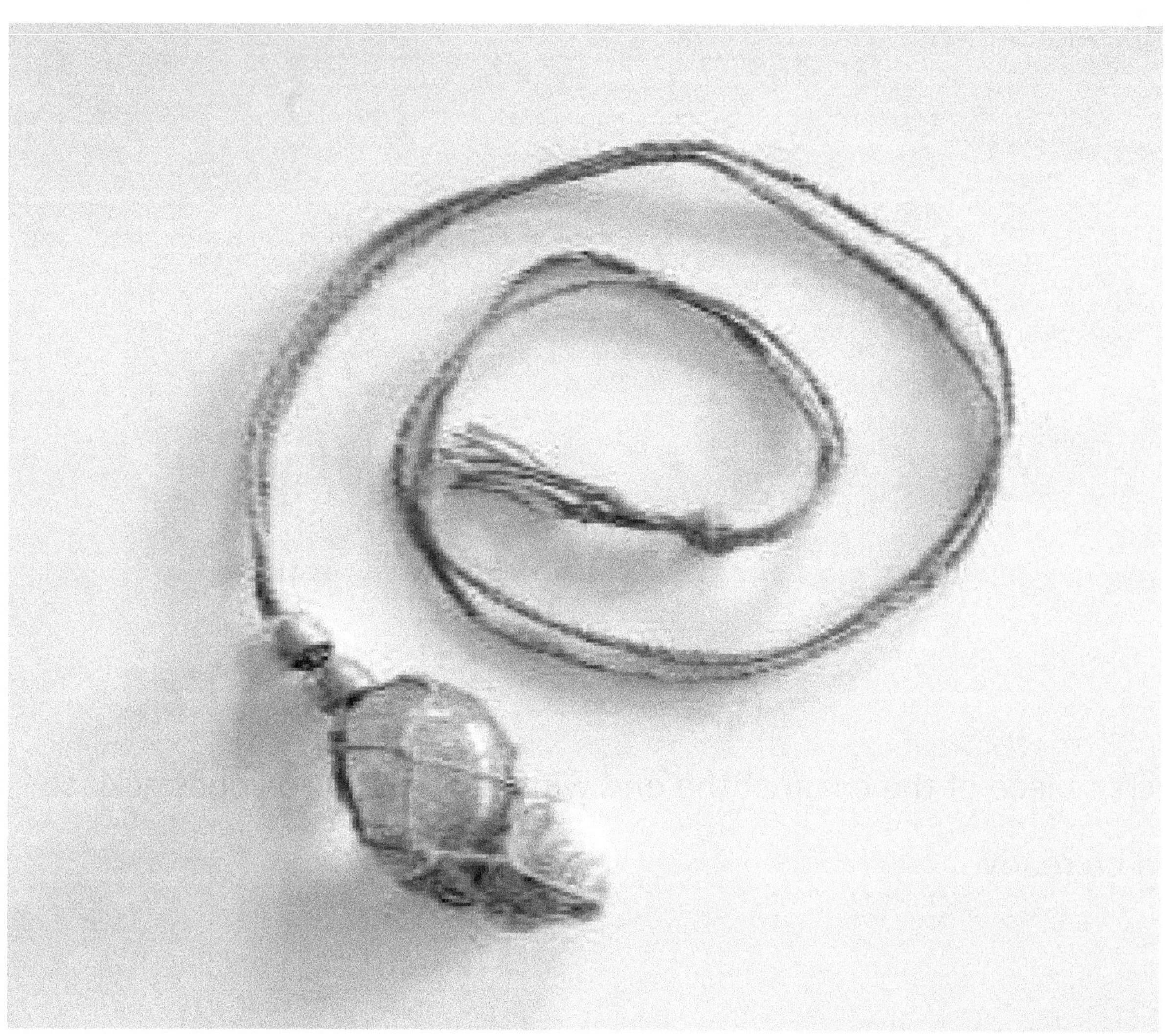

This one has that enchanting, beautiful feel! Aside from knots, it makes use of gemstones that could really spruce up your look! Surely, it's one necklace you'd love to wear over and over again!

What you need:

Your choice of gemstones

Beads

Crocheted or waxed cotton

Water

Glue

Instructions:

Get four equal lengths of cotton—this depends on how long you want the necklace to be.

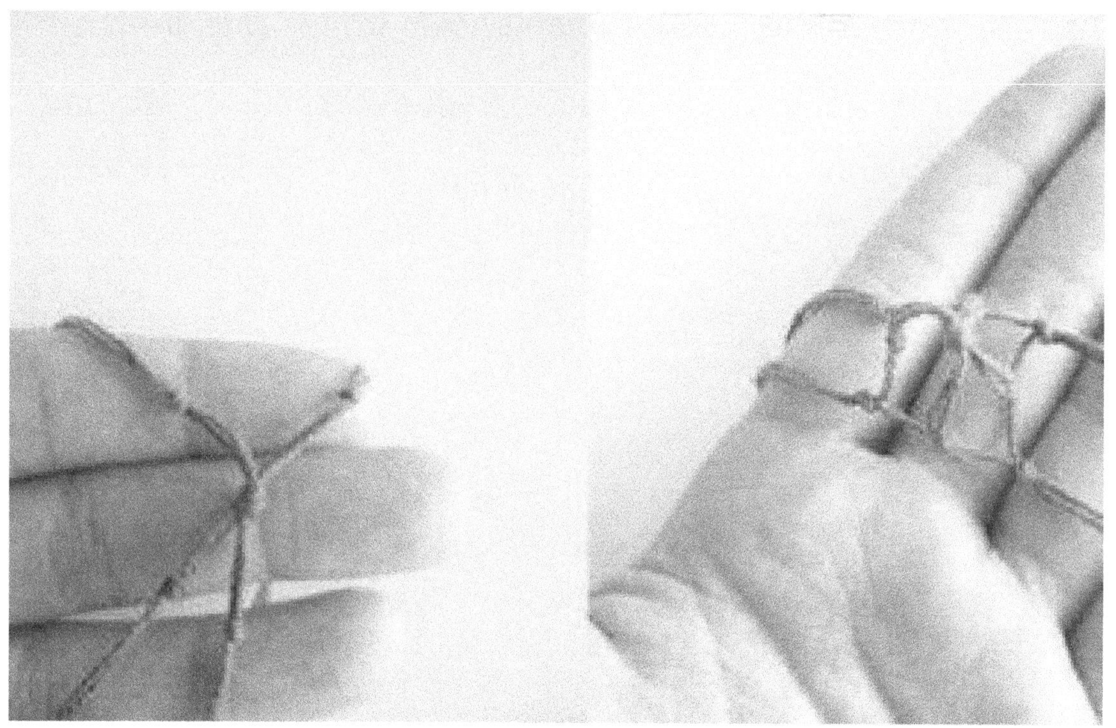

Tie a base knot as you hold the four cotton lengths. Once you do this, you'd notice that you'd have eight pieces of cotton lengths with you. What you should do is separate them into twos, and tie a knot in each of those pairs before you start knotting with the square knot.

Tie individual strands of the cotton to the length next to it. Make sure you see some depth before stringing any gemstones along, and make sure to knot before and after adding the gemstones to keep them secure.

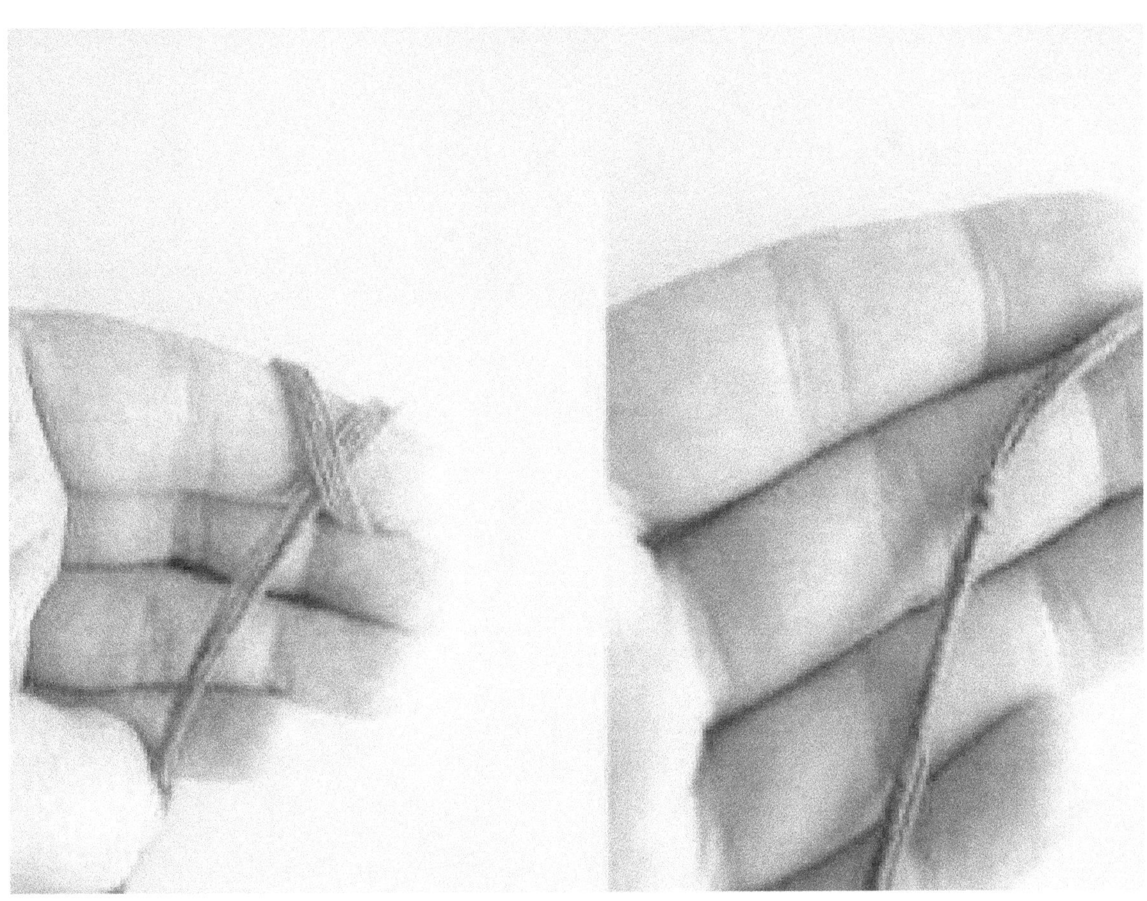

Take four of the strands in your hand and tie a knot on the top side of the bag. Tie strands until you reach the length and look you want.

Knot the ends to avoid spooling, and use water with glue to keep it more secure.

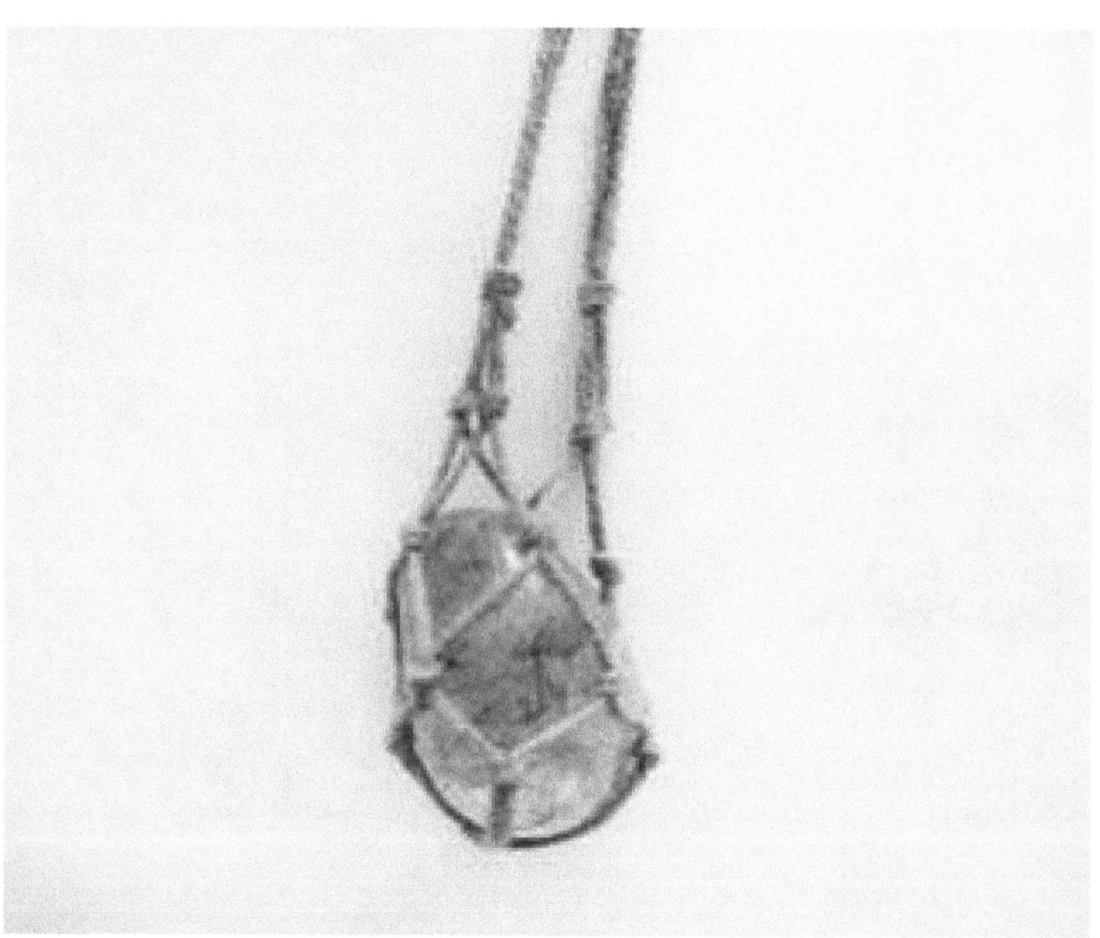

Yarn Twisted Necklace

This one is quite simple as you can use any kind of yarn that you want, especially thick or worsted ones to give your projects more flair and to make it modest—but wearable!

What you need:

Yarn in various colors

Water

Glue

Instructions:

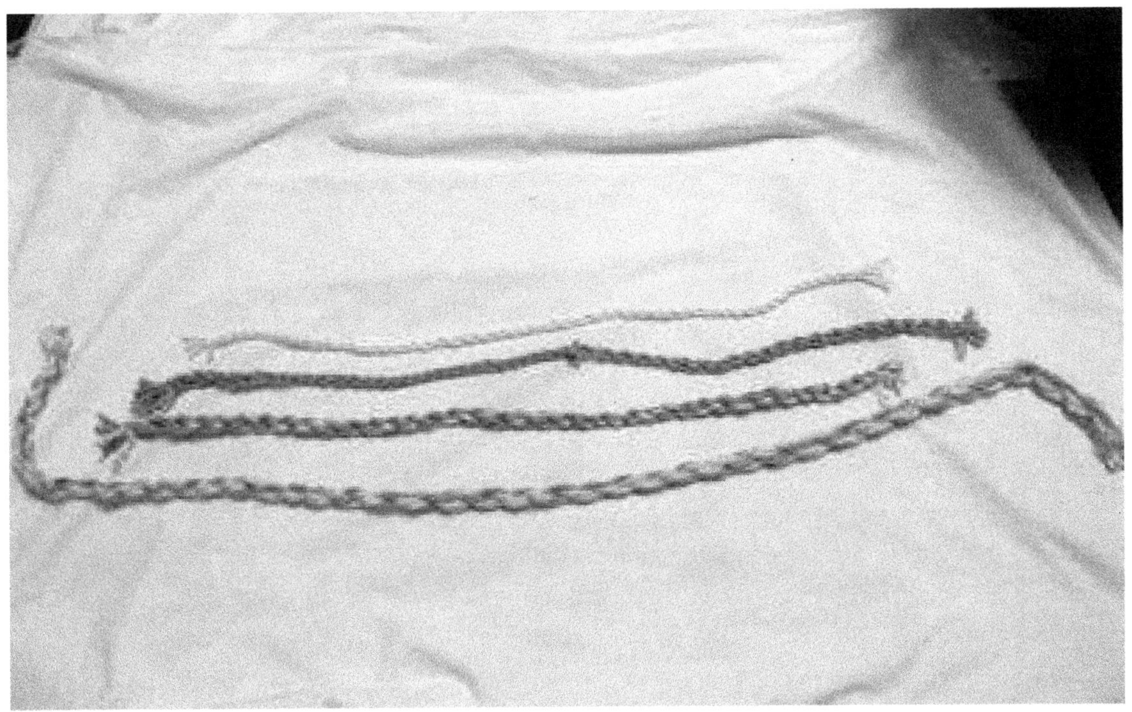

Cut two to four pieces of yarn—it's up to you how much you want.

Start braiding, and knot using the square knot. Make sure that you secure the pieces of yarn together.

Knot until your desired length, then secure the piece with a mix of glue and water at the ends.

Nautical Rope Necklace

This one is light and easy on the eyes, and is quite edgy—literally and figuratively, without being over the top! It will also remind you of the sea—or the waves of the ocean!

What you need:

Pendant with jump ring or bail

Ruler

Scissors

White nylon cord

Knotting board

Instructions:

Cut 7 feet or 84" of nylon cord.

Then, keep the strands together as a group. Tie an overhand knot around the two strings. Make sure there's 1 to 2" of space between them.

Make an overhand knot 6" away from the end. Tighten the knot by pulling individual strands and make sure to secure it on the knotting board. Separate the strands into two groups.

Take the left part of the cord and cross it under the right corner of the cord. Get the right cord group and cross it over the left side. Tighten as you pull down and knot until you reach 16 inches.

Check the last double chain and make an overhand knot. Tie them 6 inches from what you have created. Add a pendant, if you want, and make sure you knot before and after adding it to keep it secure.

Macramé Tie-Dye Necklace

This one is knotted tightly, which gives it the effect that it's strong—but still really elegant. This is a good project to craft—you'd enjoy the act of making it, and wearing it, as well!

What you need:

1 pack laundry rope

Tulip One-Step Dye

Fabric glue

Candle

Jump rings

Lobster clasp

Instructions:

Tie the rope using crown knots.

After tying, place the knotted rope inside the One-Step Dye pack (you could get this in most stores) and let it set and dry overnight.

Upon taking it out, leave it for a few hours and then secure the end of the knot with fabric glue mixed with a bit of water.

Trim the ends off and burn off the ends with wax from candle.

Add jump rings to the end and secure with lobster clasp.

Enjoy your tie-dye necklace!

Macramé Hat

This Macramé Hat has a round top and a beautifully decorated brim with tiny triangles. It can also be used as a Macramé basket.

For this, it is recommended to use a material which is not extremely flexible, or it doesn't keep its shape. Bonnie Braid is used in the illustration given below.

A medium-sized hat with dimensions of 28 inches around with a 1.5-inch brim will be created here. If you want to make a smaller or larger hat, I have provided you with cord measurements.

It is a simple project for beginners. Be sure to practice the decorative knots stated under before you attempt to make this personalized hat if you're new to Macramé.

Materials Required:

- 4mm Cord Material (114 yards)
- Fabric Glue
- Tape Measure
- Pins and Project Board

Knots used:

- Alternating Square Knots (ASK)
- Larks Head Knot
- Overhand Knot
- Double Half Hitch (DHH)

Step by Step Instructions:

1. For the hat created here, you will need to cut 56 cords, which should be 2 yards in length each. For a 24-inch hat cut one holding cord 36 inches long and 48 other strings, each of which must be 2 yards in length. For a 32-inch hat, you will need a total of 64 cords, 2.5 yards each. For a hat above or below these sizes, increase or decrease the size as needed (2 strings per inch). The number of cords you use should be multiples of 4. Fix the split ends of the cord with a tape. It would prevent the unraveling of the strings. Tie the holding string with your work station horizontally, and make sure it is stretched firmly. Fold in half one of the two yard strings, and place it under the holding string, so that it lies near the center.

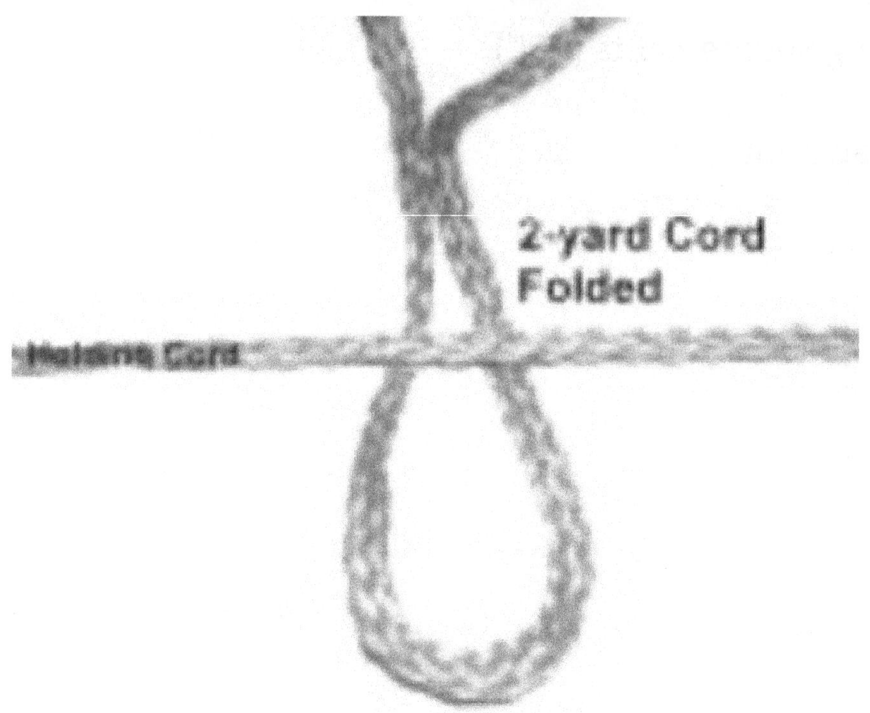

2. Place the ends over the holding cord to complete the formed Larks Head knot, going downward. Move them underneath the folded line. Stiffly close.

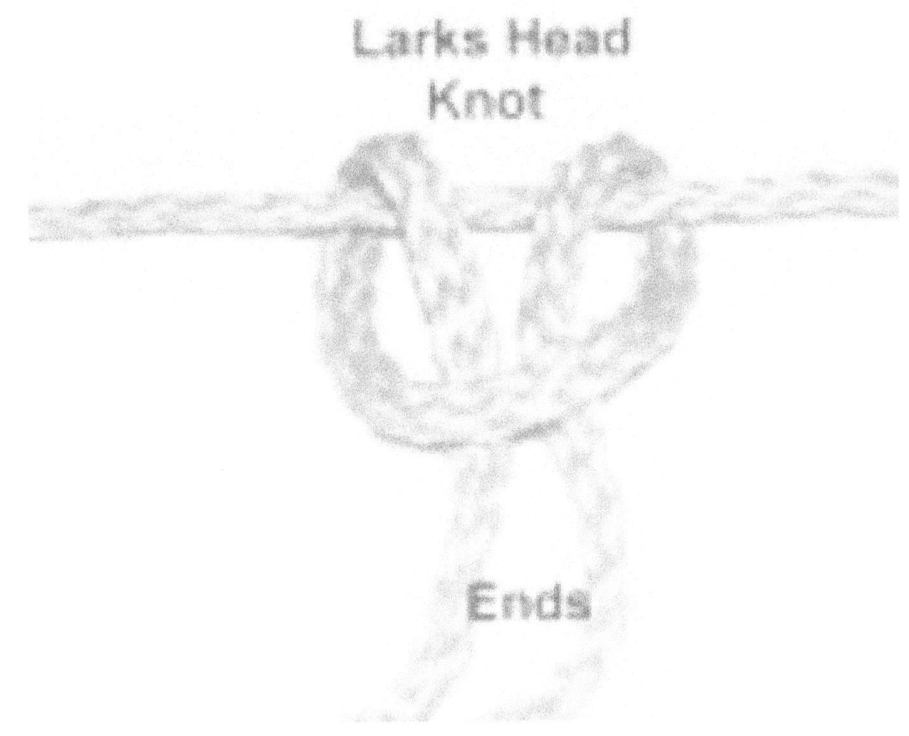

3. Attach each end of Half Hitch knot by leading the rope over and below the holding string. It will ride over the thread you're working with when you set it down.

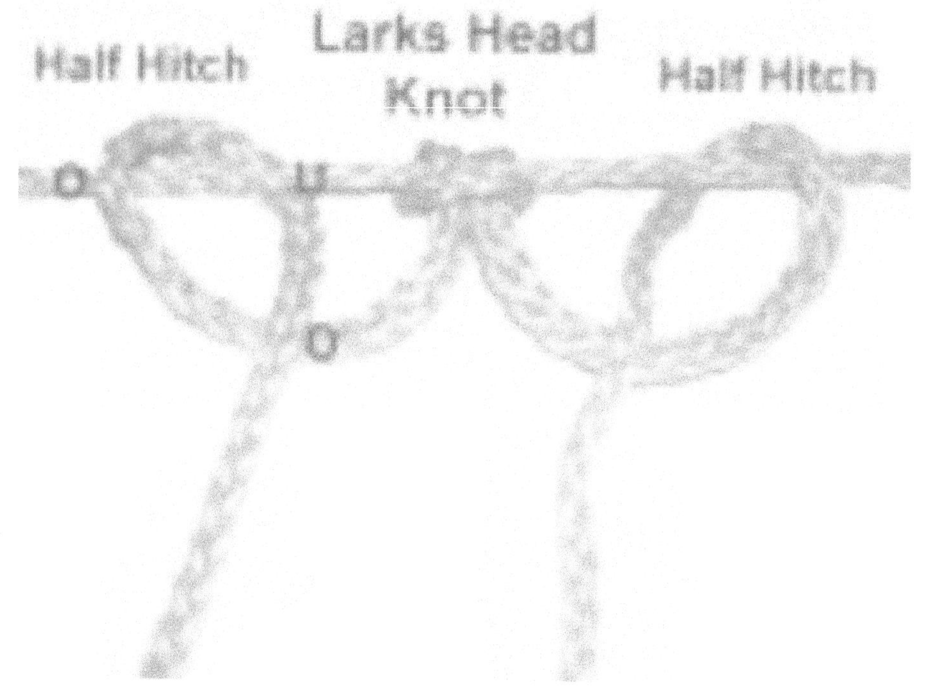

4. Repeat the steps from step 1 to 3, by wrapping the remaining strings to your holding string. Start working from the center and move to the ends. There must be an equivalent amount of strings in both directions.

5. For creating the edge for your Macramé Hat, chose any eight cords and marked them from cord 1 to 8 from left towards right. All the triangle designs are created using eight strings, so split them out now, before you start working on the triangles. Make a Square Knot with 2-4 strings. You only have one filler

the string 3. Tightly firm it, so it sets against your mounted knots. Do it again with the strings 5, 6, and 7. This time the filler is cord 6.

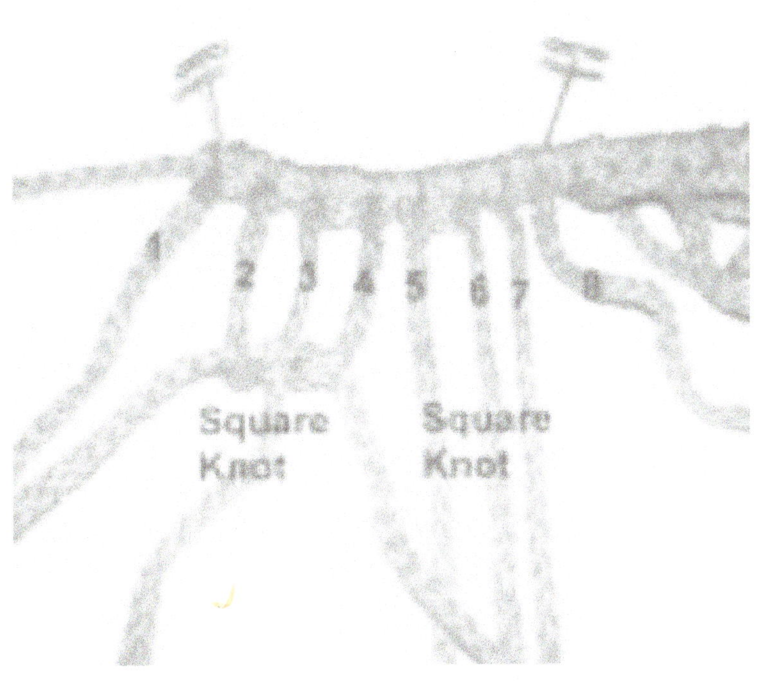

6. Now attach the other Square Knot under the first two, using strings 3 - 6 (two fillers -- 4 and 5). Tighten the knots firmly, so it rests over the knots above it.

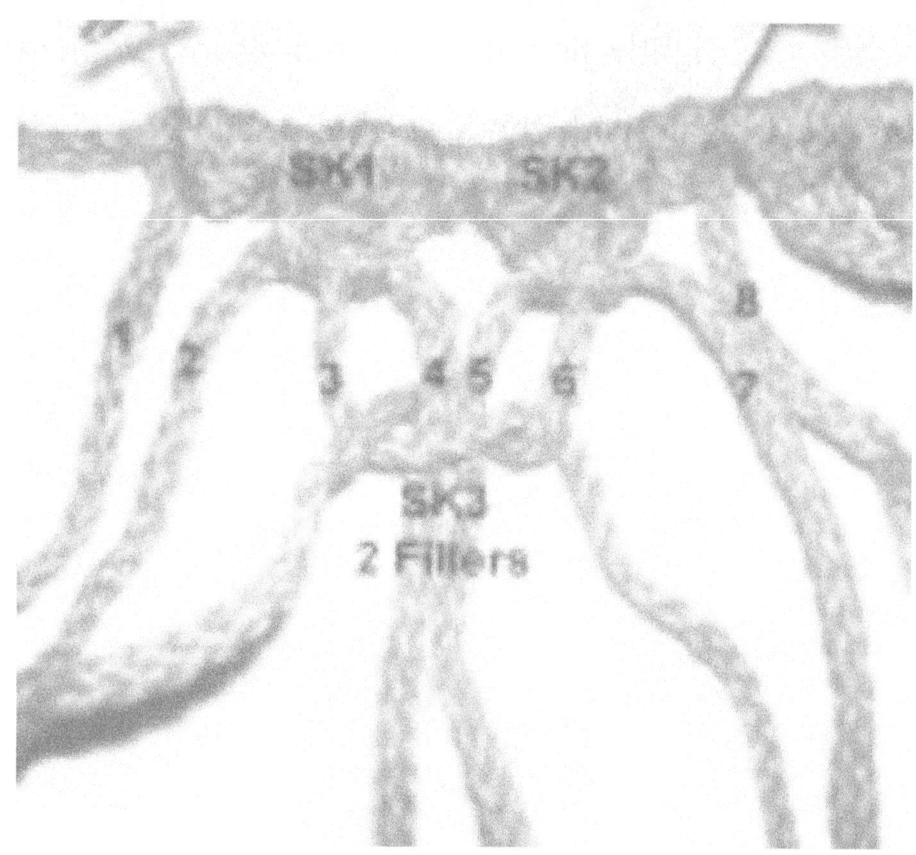

7. Move the cord number 1 with the left side of the three knots that forms a triangular shape. Lock it, so that it's tight since it is a holding string. Join the cords 2, 3, and 4 to it through the Double Half Hitches.

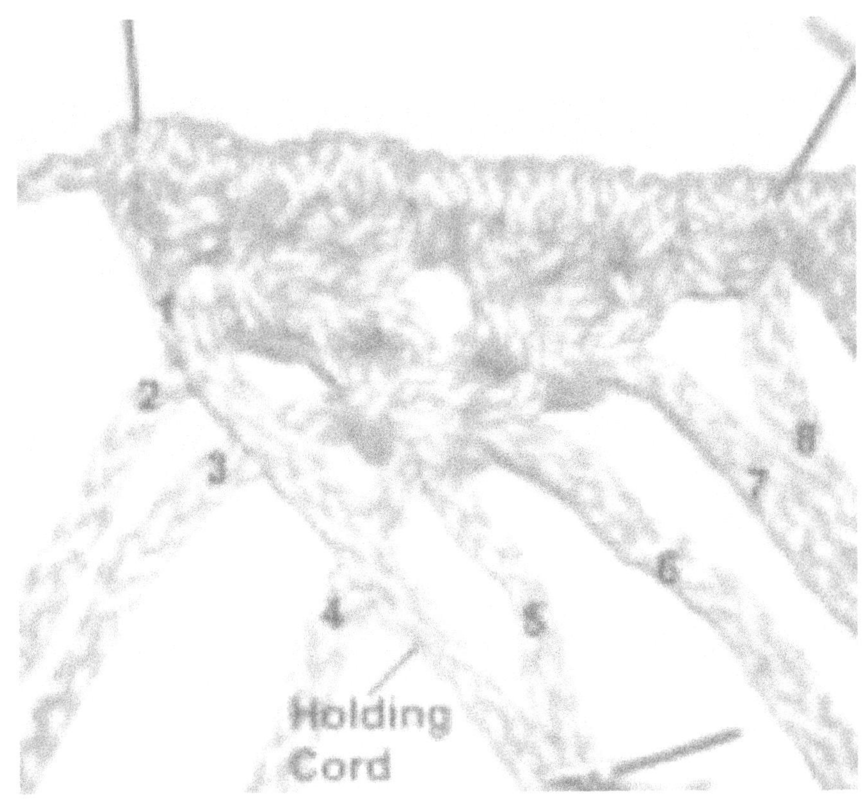

8. Move the string 8 along the right edge of the triangle, and fix it as well. Attach strings 5, 6, and 7 with it with a Double Half Hitch knot. Make sure not to attach the holding cord 1 with it, or the design will be unbalanced.

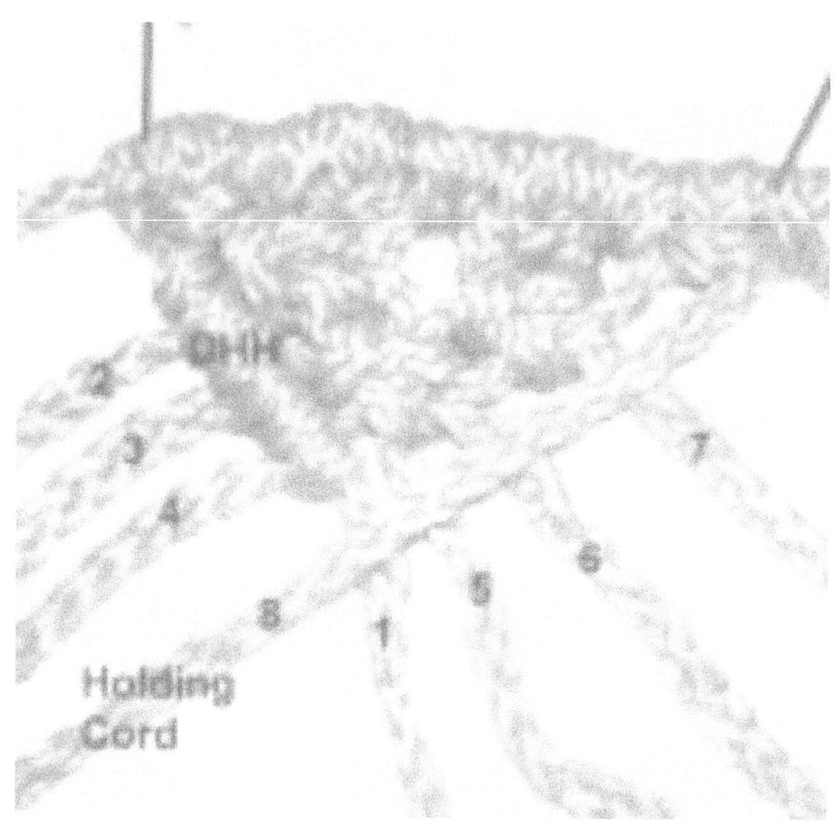

9. Make a cross using the firming string 1 and 8, and extent all the strings in a manner so it will be easier for you to see them. Attach a Square Knot using cords 1, 4, 5, and 8. Use cords 8 and 1 as the fillers. Firmly tie the knots, so that the knot stays below triangle level.

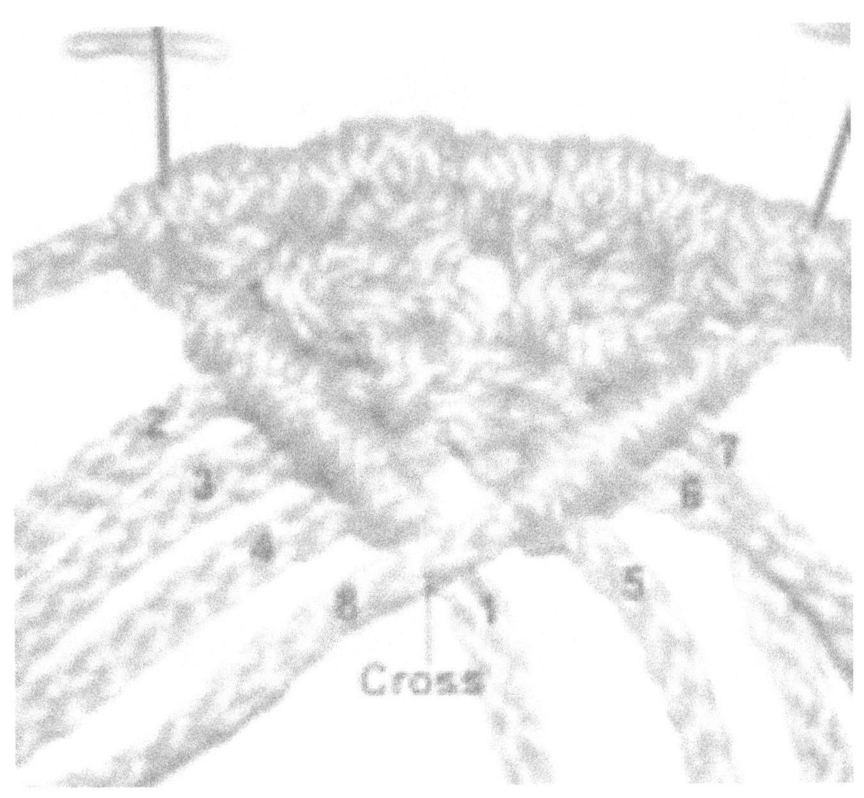

10. Repeat steps 5 to 9, to make additional triangle with the help of your next eight cords. Attach a Square Knot from the first line, with cords 6 and 7, and 2 and 3 from the second side. Tighten it so under each triangle it meets up with the Square Knot.

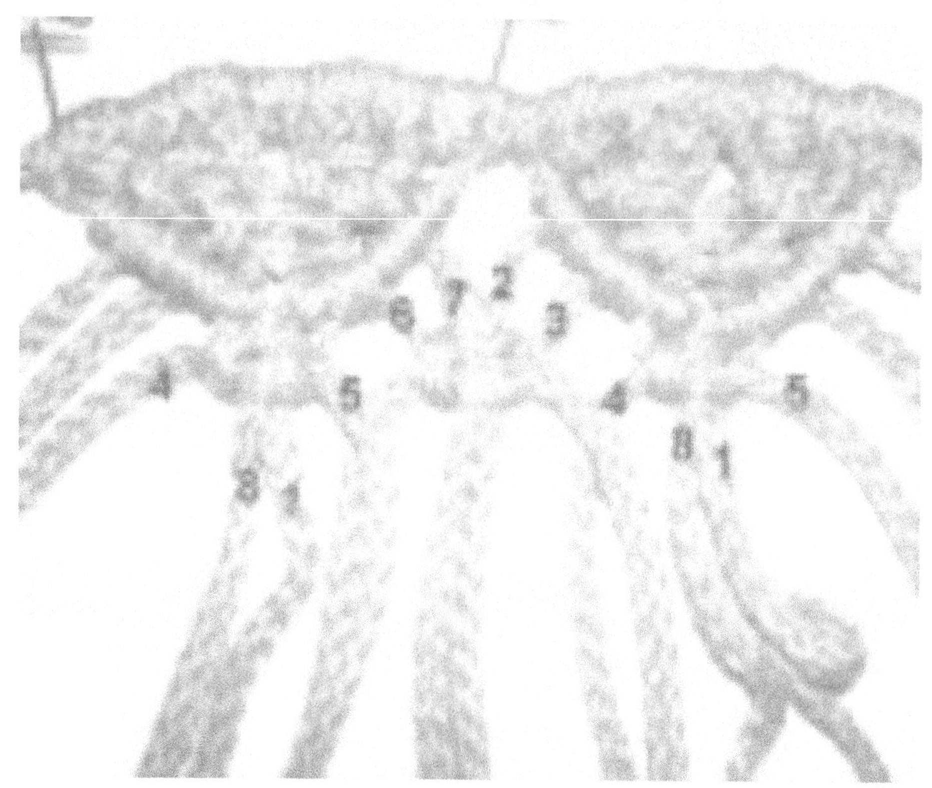

11. Repeat step from step no 5 to 10 with the help of remaining clusters of cords. When you reach the final triangle figure for your Macramé Hat, connect this triangle to the first triangle you created, to make a complete circle. Now begin turning upside down the brim of your Macramé Cap. Although actually the right side of the triangles is on the opposite side of the hat.

12. Keep in mind that the brim which is created will be folded in a manner, so the orders are swapped. It can be also be seen in the picture attached below, which is showing the rear side of the triangles at the moment, where you will be doing your work. Attach

a Square Knot with the help of strings 2 and 3 from the first triangle that you created, with 6 and 7 from the last triangle.

13. It is just what you have done in the last step, and the only difference is that the cords come from each edge of the brim

Identify the edges of your holding string used in the tying process. Once you identify your holding cord, tie an Overhand knot and glue it, and tie another one on the upper side of the first knot. Trim the excess by 2 inches, fold them under the mounting knots, and apply a generous amount of glue so it holds the knots in its place. Don't forget that the triangles should be at the back side and not on the front.

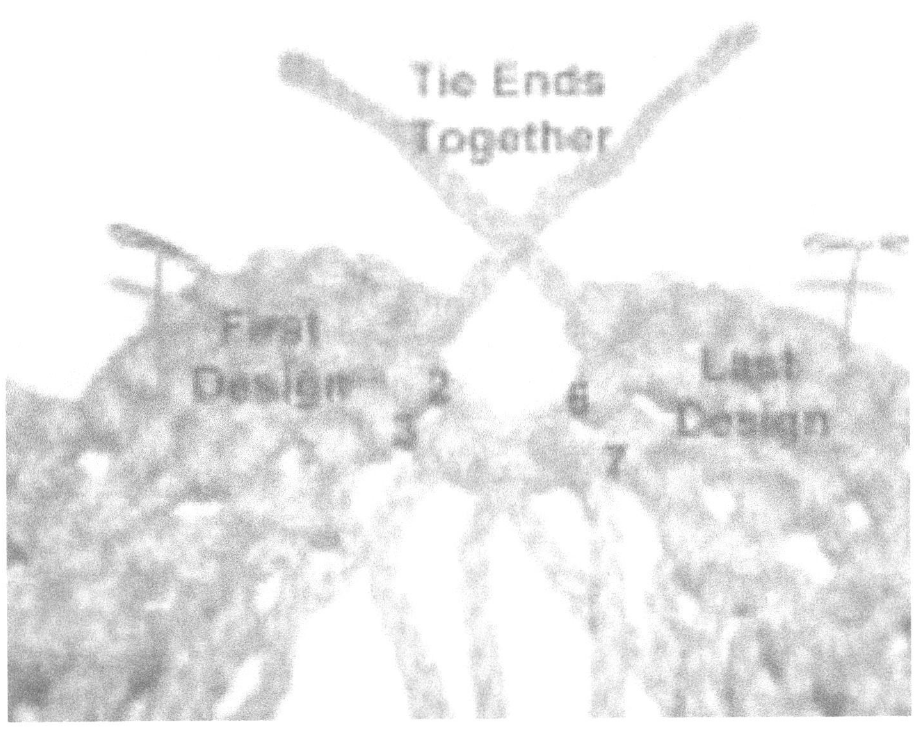

12. To create the top part, you will link a row of Alternating Square knots (ASK) using 4 cords per knot, two working cords, and two fillers. Starting at the place where the two ends were connected in phase 7 is easiest, then continuing around the entire route. To create the next row, alternate the strings. Keep the brim on the inner side while creating your hat. Mentally number each set with four cords. Strings No.1 and No.4 act as the working cords, while two and three are the filler cords. Combine 3 and 4 with 1 and 2 from next knot over to alternate for next lines. And the current knot lies between the two above.

13. Stop tying Alternating Square Knot when your Macramé hat is at least 7 inches in height which starts from the lower end of the brim, till the row of knots that you are currently working on. Keep in mind you'll cover the bottom, so you'll only have a couple more rows to add to the top.

14. Choose 12 cords that are coming from the three Alternating Square Knots. Visually mark each set with four cords as A, B, and C. Push all the four strings from the set B to the inside of the Macramé hat.

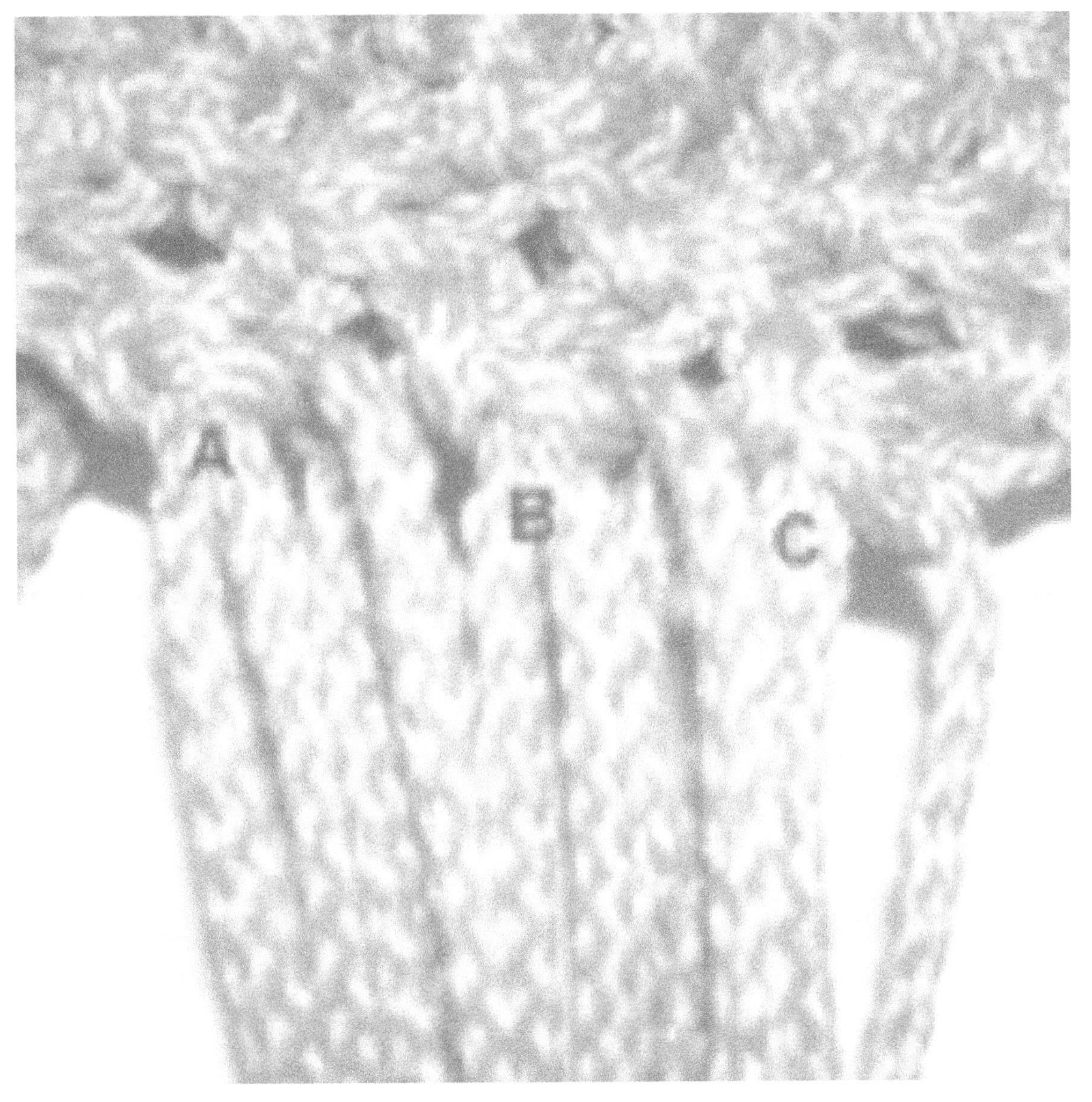

15. Use the cords 3 and 4 from set A (that is at the extreme left side), with strings No.1 and No.2 from your set C (that is at the extreme right side). With these four ropes, tie securely a Square Knot over the gap left by the strings you just put through. Tighten the knots firmly. So the top edge of your hat will appear more rounded.

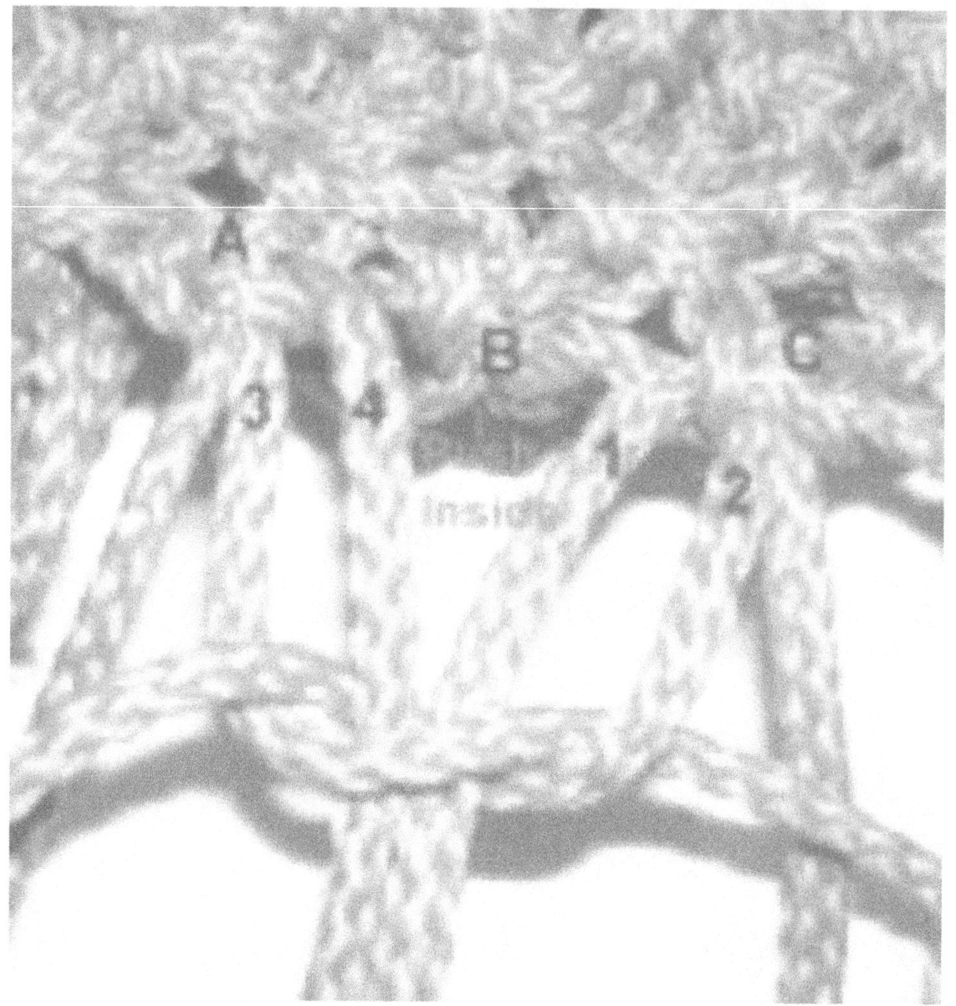

16. Repeat the step by dropping all the remaining knots by pushing the knots inside. This will fasten the top of the Macramé Hat. Do steps 3 and 4 two more times, until you've been all the way back. Move the remaining cords into the inside until you are done.

17. Take the right side of the hat up. Note, that the front of the triangles at the top is the bottom, and while you're focusing on these final stages, they can be seen around the lower lip. Tie two very tight

overhead knot using two cords at a time but from two different knots. If there are some wide gaps, begin crossing the void by choosing cords from each side of it. Hook one knot, apply adhesive to the thread, then tie the knot next.

18. Trim the excess cords after you tie the knots. As the strings are taped at the ends, you can simply cut them off to identify which cords are used. After you are done with tying all the knots, let the glue dry and cut off any extra material. Switch the Designer Hat's brim outwards, arrange it at the triangular tip.

Amazing Macramé Curtain

Macramé Curtains give your house the feel of that beach house look. You don't even have to add any trinkets or shells—but you can, if you want to. Anyway, here's a great Macramé Curtain that you can make!

What you need:

- Laundry rope (or any kind of rope/cord you want)
- Curtain rod
- Scissors
- Pins
- Lighter
- tape

Instructions:

Tie four strands together and secure the top knots with pins so they could hold the structure down.

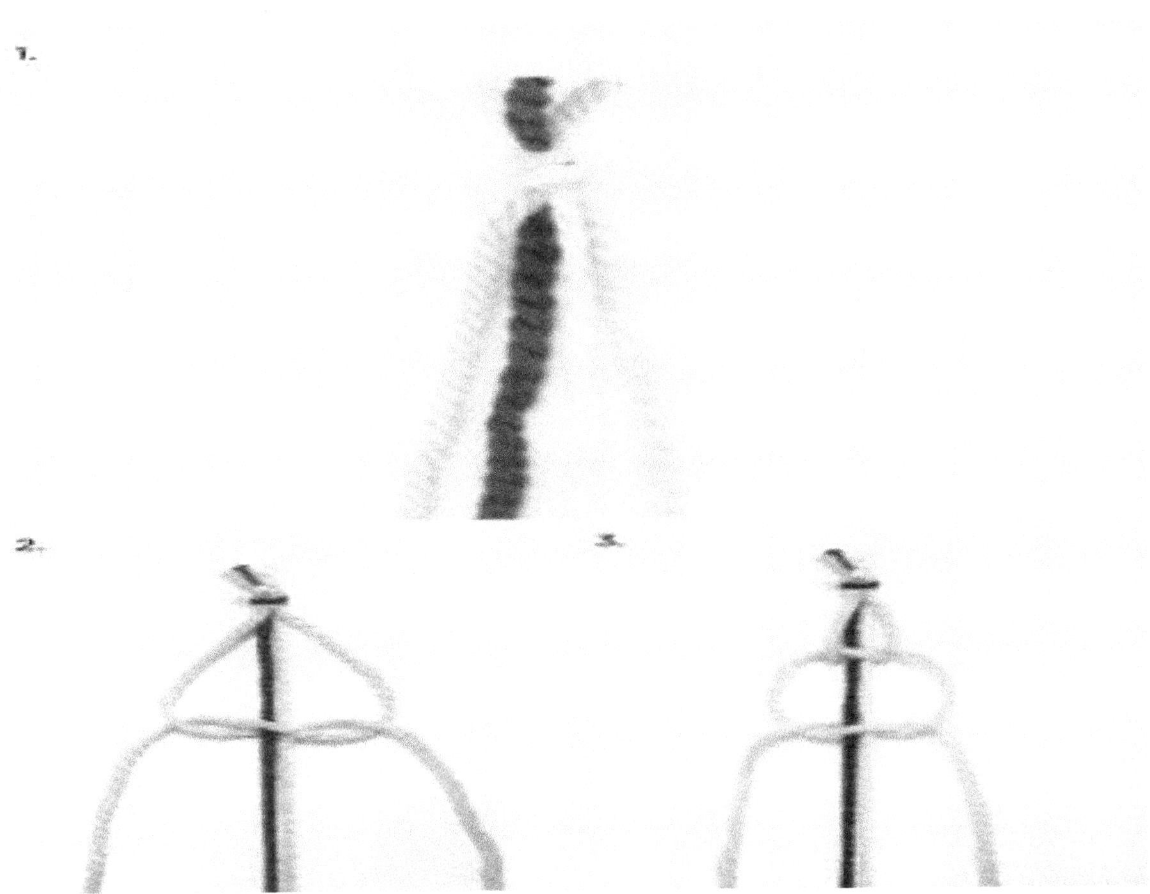

Take the strand on the outer right part and let it cross over to the left side by means of passing it through the middle. Tightly pull the strings together and reverse.

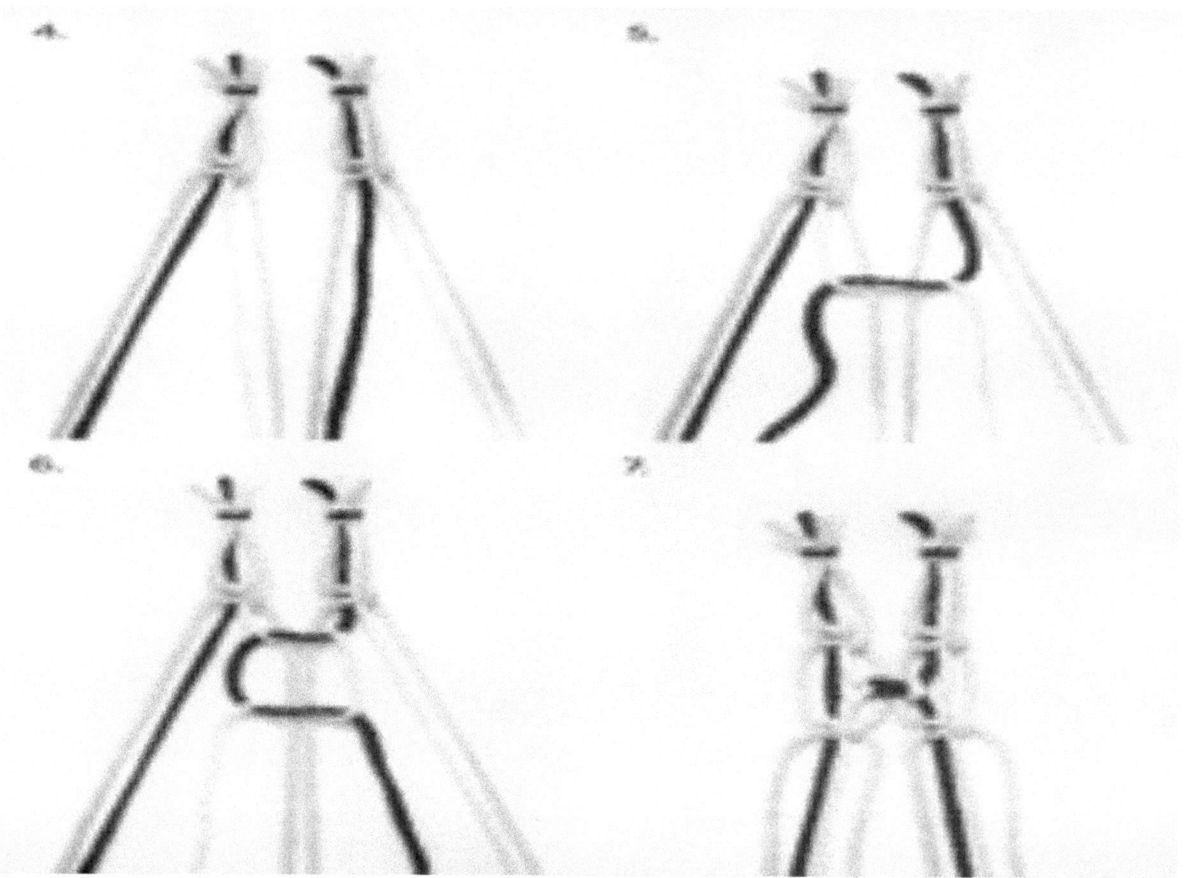

Repeat crossing the thread over four more times for the thread you now have in front of you. Take the strand on the outer left and let it pass through the middle, and then take the right and let it cross over the left side. Repeat as needed, then divide the group of strands to the left, and also to the right. Repeat until you reach the number of rows you want.

You can now apply this to the ropes. Gather the number or ropes you want—10 to 14 is okay, or whatever fits the rod, with good spacing. Start knotting at the top of the curtain until you reach your desired length. You can burn or tape the ends to prevent them from unraveling.

Braid the ropes together to give them that dreamy, beachside effect, just like what you see below.

That's it, you can now use your new curtain!

Macramé Wall Hanging

A macramé wall suspended in a home

A macramé wall hanging is an easy DIY project which adds a handmade touch to every room in your home.

Given its size, this is a simple project that takes you an hour or two to finish. It gets together quickly, and you will find many ways of adding your style.

This is only one of many free macramé patterns including plant hangers, bookmarks, curtains and much more.

The knots you use to mount this macramé wall include the head knot, the spiral knot and the square knot.

What you will need to finish this macramé DIY hanging wall:

Cotton Macramé cord (200 feet) and 61 meters (3/4-inch circumference, 24) "wooden dwell (3/4, "24-inch) scissors I've been using cotton clothesline on my macramé string. It looks entirely natural and is quite cheap.

The wooden dowel must not be such exact measurements and use whatever scale you like in place of the wood dowel as long as all ropes are placed over it. If you want to give it an outdoor experience, you can use a branch of a tree about the same height.

Make a hanger for your wooden dowel

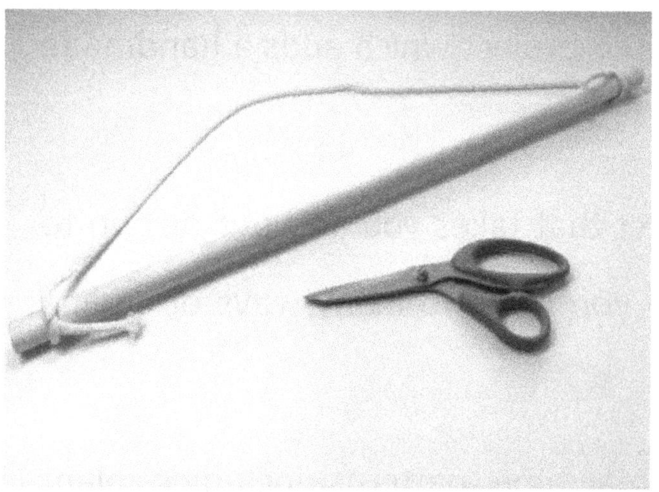

Cut a piece of macramé cord that is three feet (1 meter) and tied to a wooden dowel. Connect the two sides of the wooden dowel to each end of the thread. You are going to use this to mount your macramé project when it is over. In the beginning, I like to attach it, so I can hang up the macramé project when I tie knots. It is much easier to work this way than to determine it.

Cut your macramé rope into 12 string lengths 15 feet (4.5 meters) long with the pair of scissors. It might sound like a lot of rope, but knots take up more cord than you expect. If you need it, there's no way to make the rope thicker, so you better cut it than you will.

Fold one of the macramé cores in half on the wooden dowel and use a ladle's head knot to tie it to a wooden dowel

Join the other cords in the same way

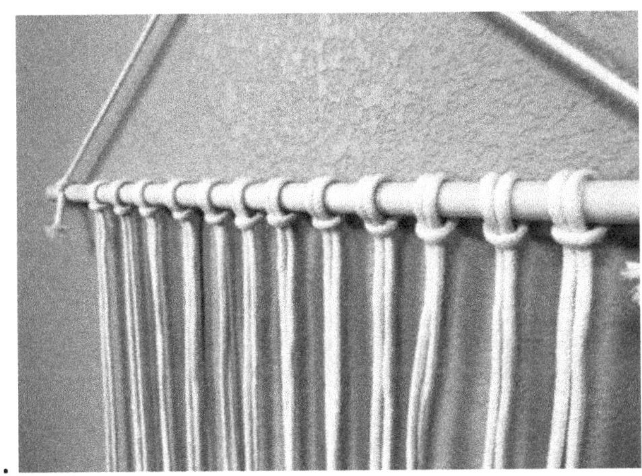

.

Take the first four strings and make left facing spiral stitch (also referred to as a half-knot Lynton) by tying 13 half knots.

Using four rope to make a further spiral stitch of 13 half knots using the same pair of four ropes. Continue to work in four-chord sections. You should have a minimum of six spiral stitches before you finish.

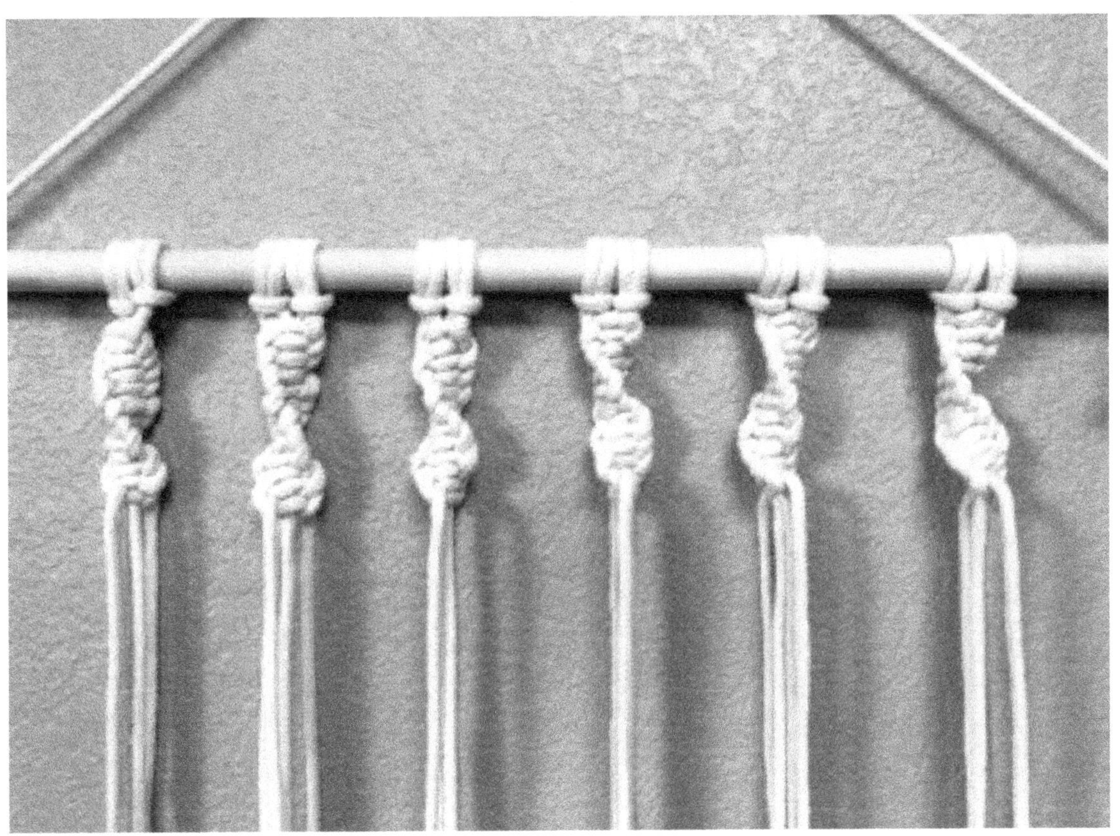

Scale about two inches down from the last knot in a spiral point. This is where your next knot, the square knot, will be found.

Make a right knot profile with the first four strings. Continue to make the correct knots face throughout this row. Do your best to keep them all even horizontally. You're going to end up with six knots together.

The second row of square knots Now is the time to start the square knots so we can have the knots "V" shape

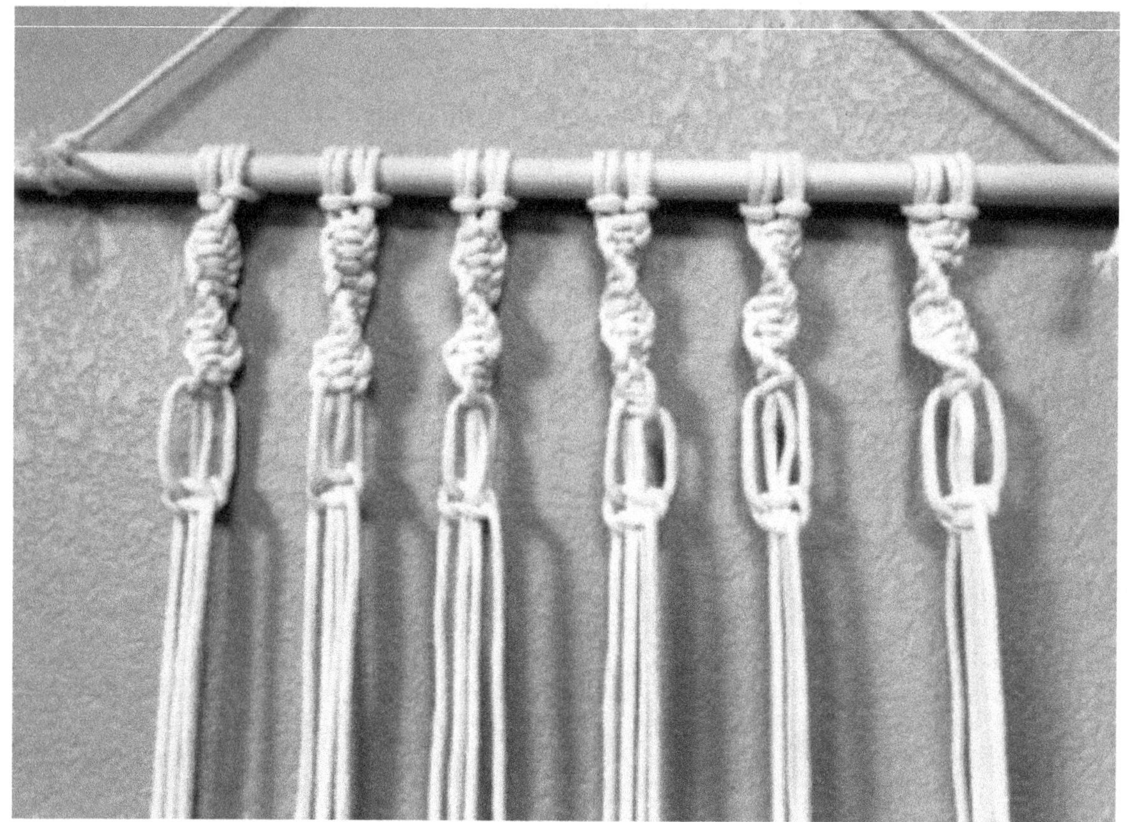

.

Set open the first two strings and the last two strings. Consider each group of four right-facing square knots. You now have a second line with the first two and last two unknotted cords and five square knots. It doesn't matter how you space them; just keep them for each row together.

Keep Decreasing the Square knots A "V" formed from the square knots in the third row, the first four strings and the last four strings will be left out. You're going to have four knots together. For the fourth row at the top, leave six cords and at the end six cords. You're going to have 3 square ties. In the fifth row, in the beginning, you'll have eight cords and at the end eight cords. Now you're going to have two square ties. For the sixth and final row, ten cords at the beginning and ten cords at the end are to be released. It lets you make a last square knot with four strings.

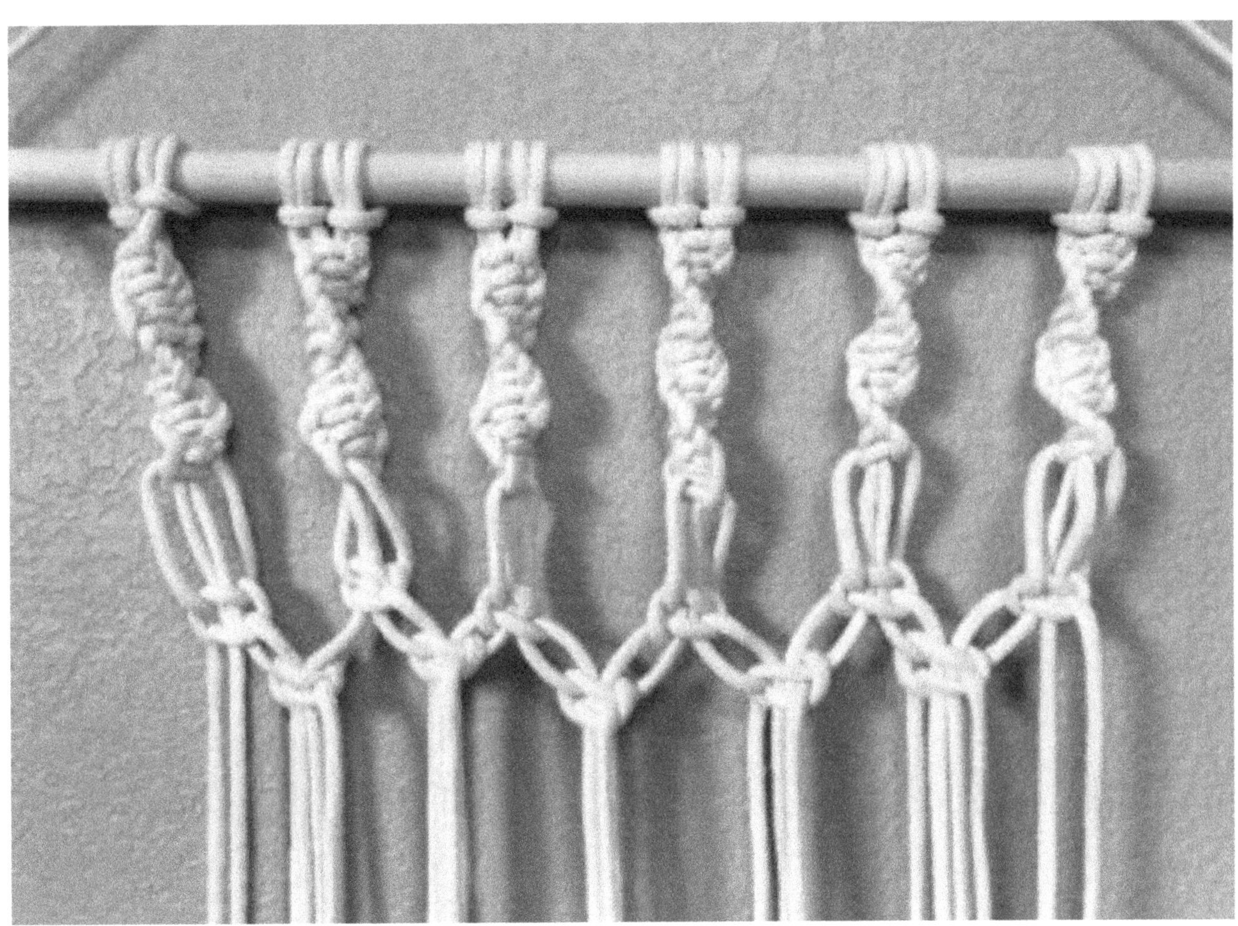

Square Knots Square Making a second "V' in square knots Next time we'll increase them into a triangle or an upside-down" V "For this section's first segment, bring out the first eight and last eight cords. That will make two square knots.

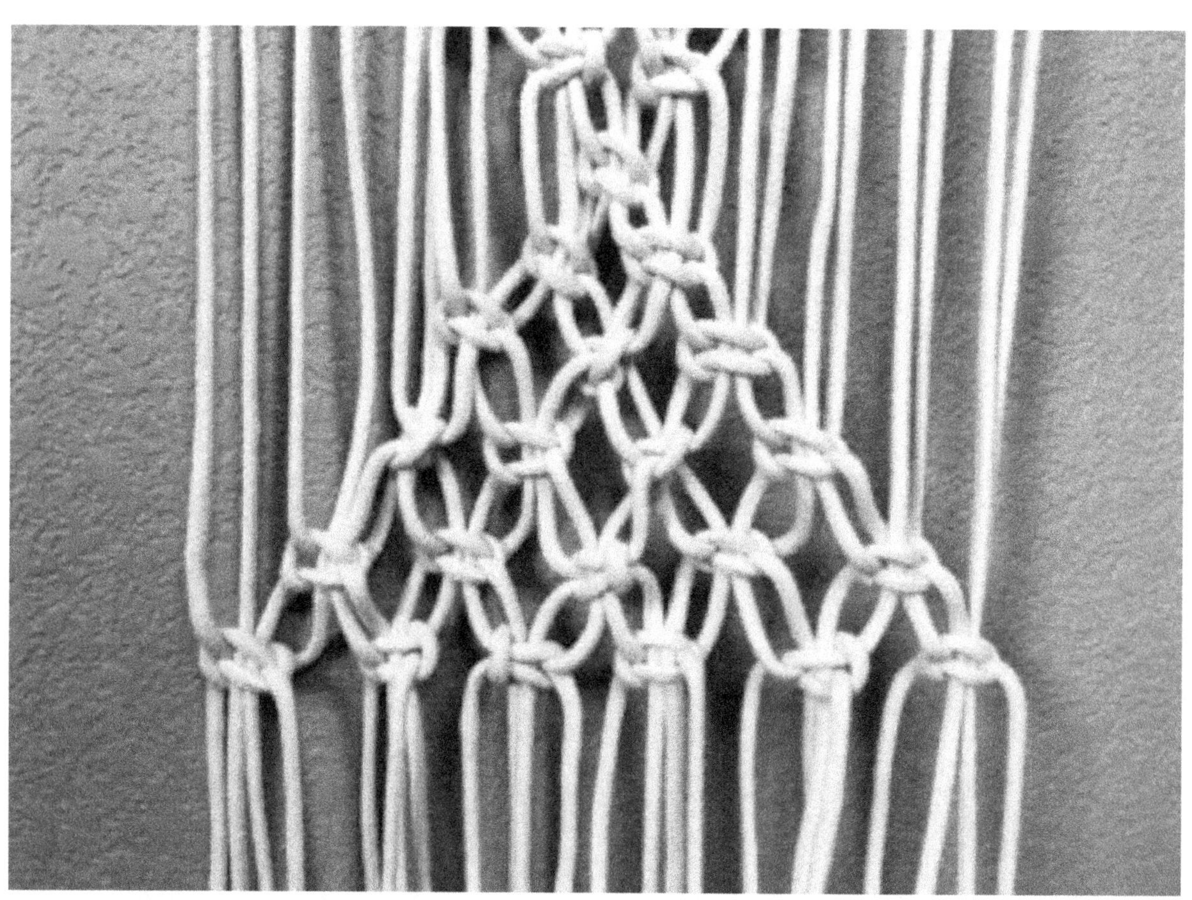

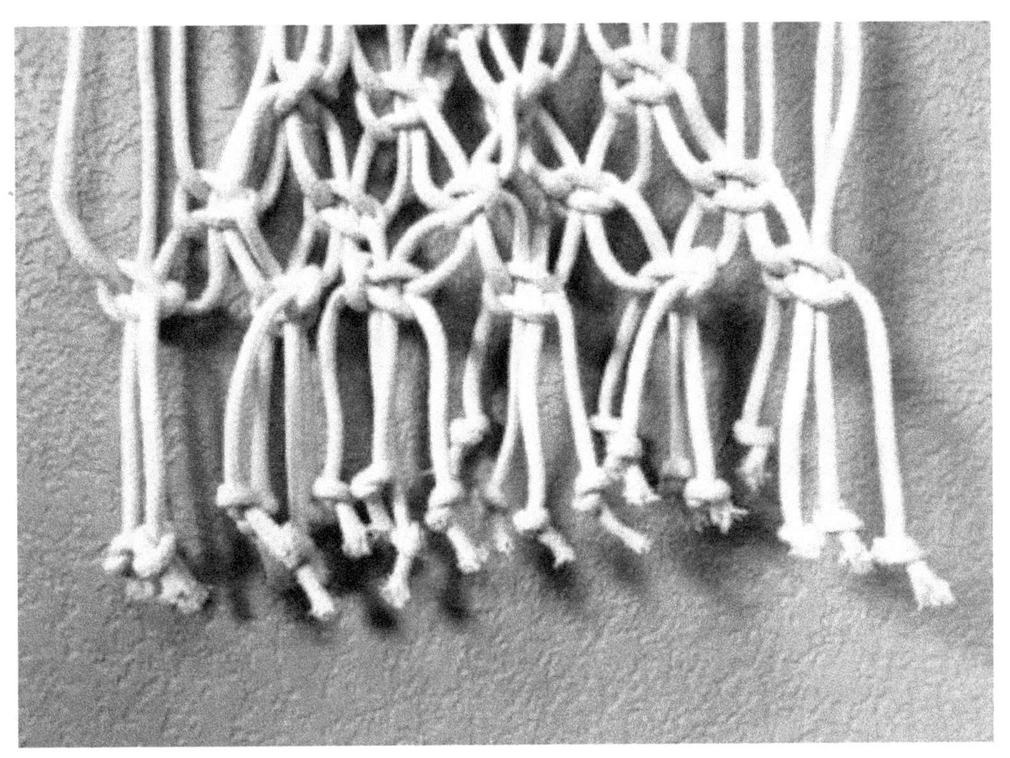

Macramé Charm and Feather Décor

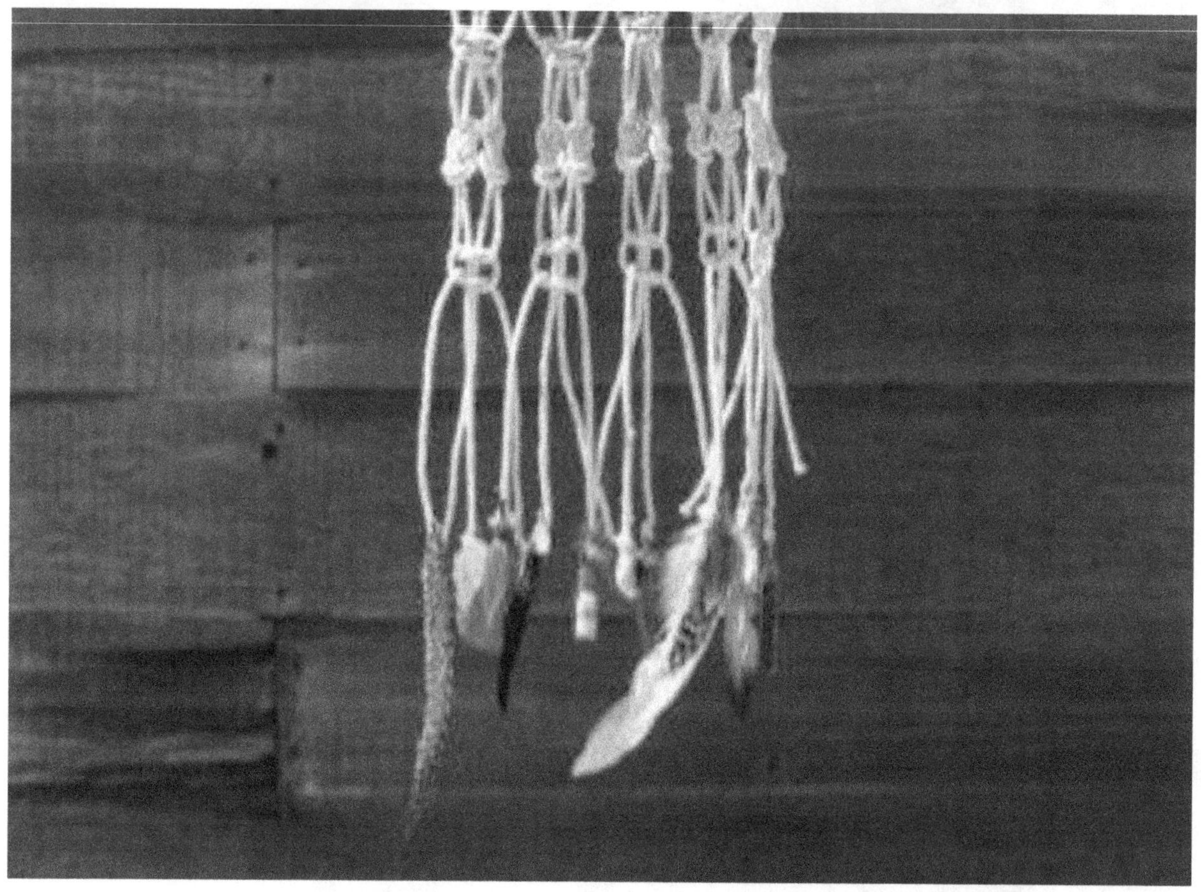

Charms and feathers always look cool. They just add a lot of that enchanting feeling to your house and knowing that you could make Macramé décor with charms and feathers really take your crafting game to new heights! Check out the instructions below and try it out for yourself!

What you need:

- Stick/dowel
- feathers and charms with holes (for you to insert the thread in)
- Embroidery/laundry rope (or any other rope or thread that you want)

Instructions:

Cut as many as you want of pieces rope as you want. Around 10 to 12 pieces is good, and then fold each in half. Make sure to create a loop at each end, like the ones you see below:

Then, go and loop each piece of thread on the stick.

Make use of the square knot and make sure you have four strands for each knot. Let the leftmost strand cross the two strands and then put it over the strands that you have in the middle. Tuck it under the middle two, as well.

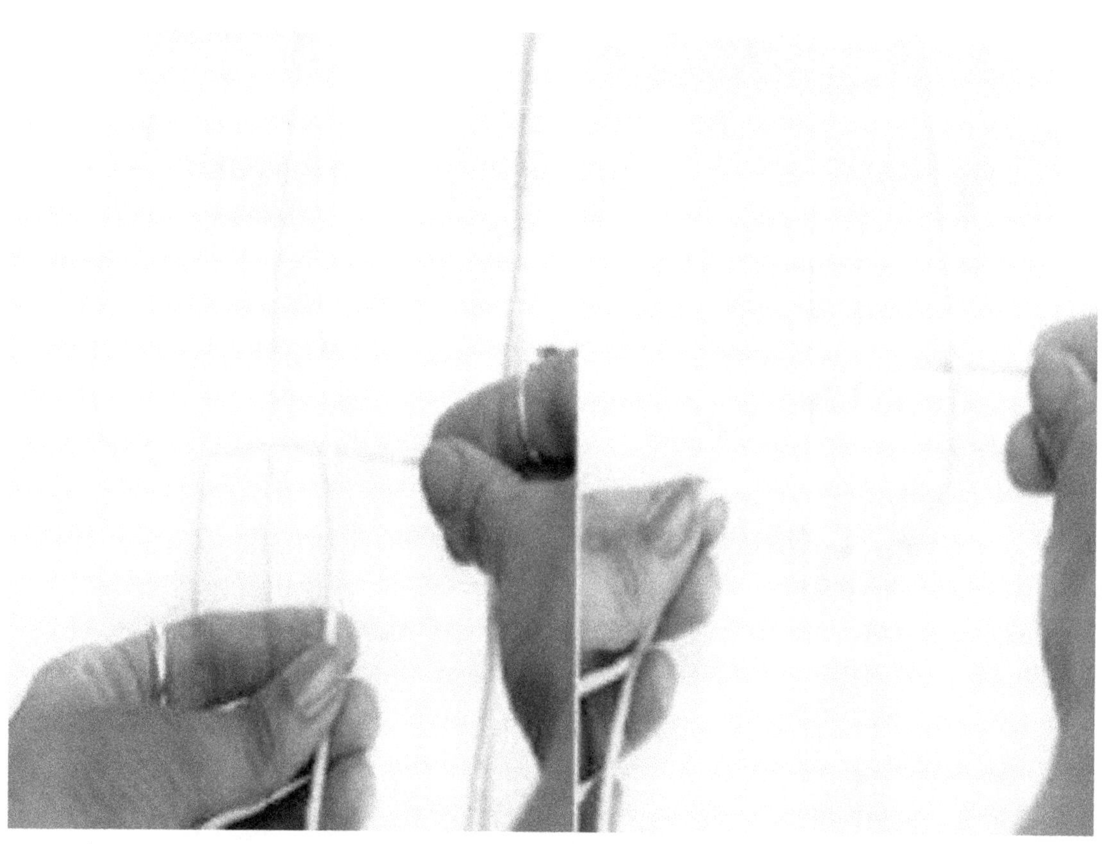

Check under the strands and let the rightmost strand be tucked under the loop to the left-hand strand.

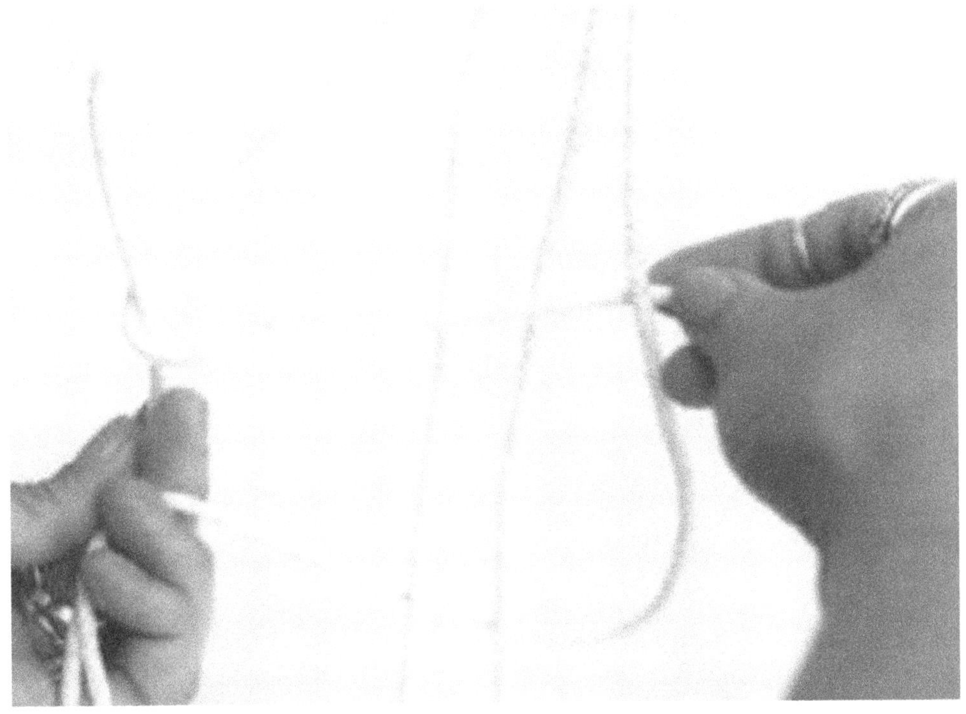

Tighten the loop by pulling the outer strands together and start with the left to repeat the process on the four strands. You will then see that a square knot has formed after tightening the loops together.

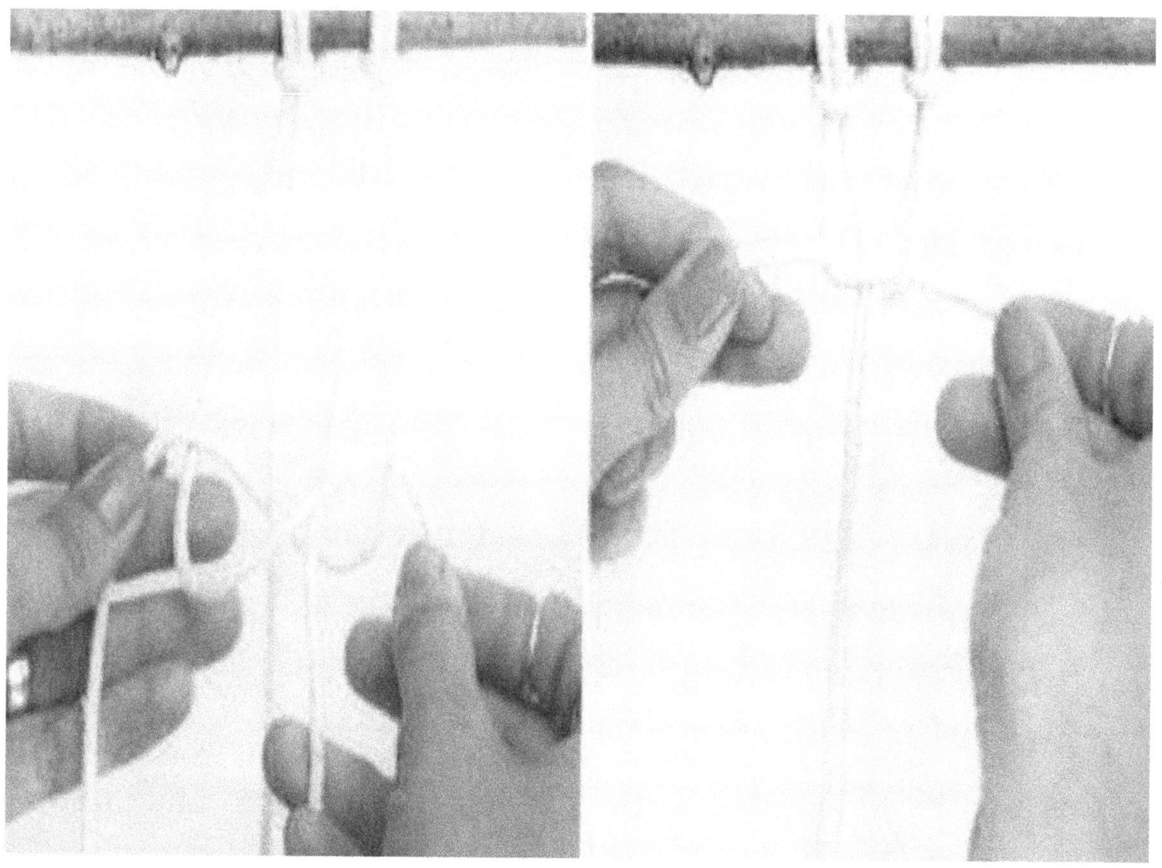

Connect the strands together by doing square knots with the remaining four pieces of rope and then repeat the process again from the left side. Tighten the loop by pulling the outer strands together and start

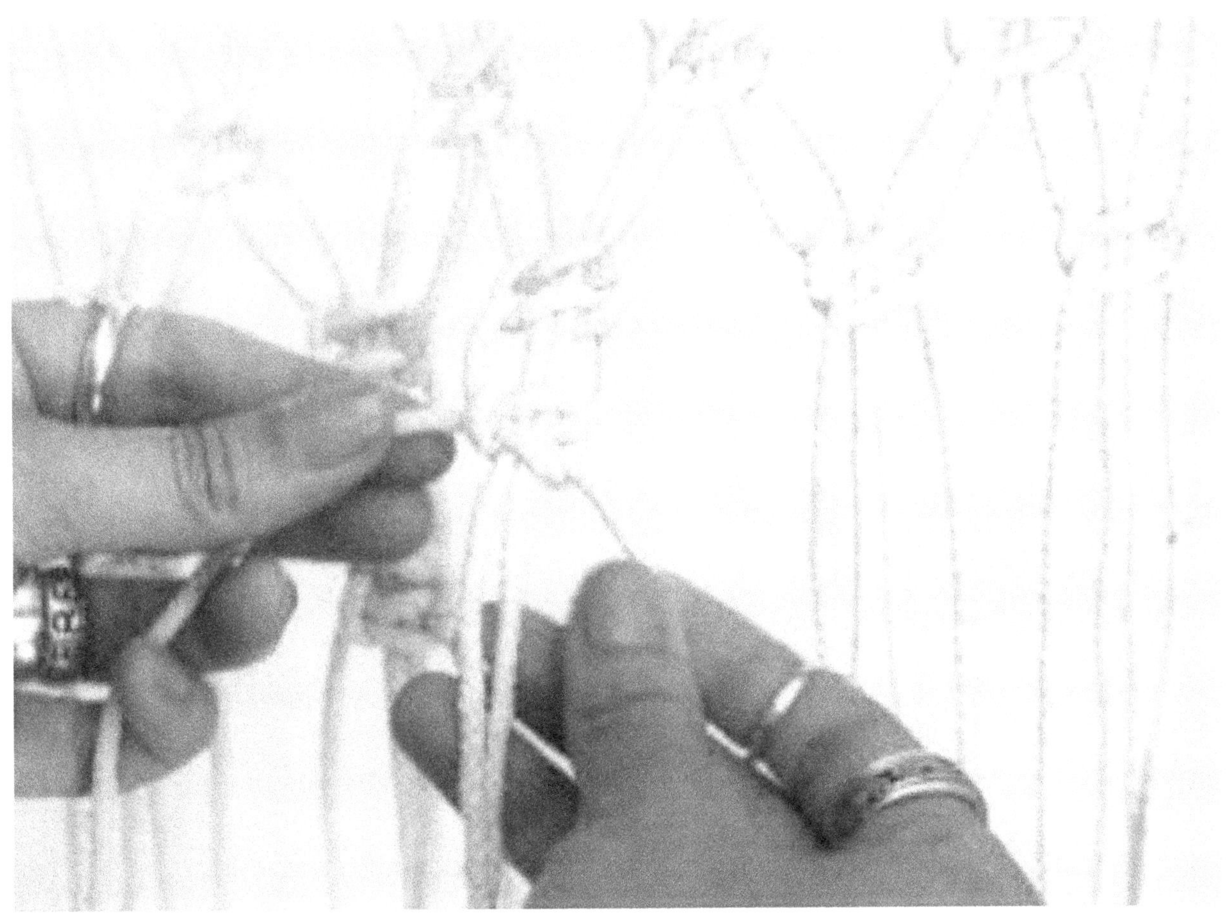

with the left to repeat the process on the four strands. You will then see that a square knot has formed after loops have been tightened together.

You can then do a figure eight knot and then just attach charms and feathers to the end. Glue them in and burn the ends for better effect!

Macramé Wall Art

Adding a bit of Macramé to your walls is always fun because it livens up the space without making it cramped—or too overwhelming for your taste. It also looks beautiful without being too complicated to make. You can check it out below!

What you need:

- Large wooden beads
- Acrylic paint
- Painter's tape
- Scissors
- Paintbrush
- Wooden dowel
- 70 yards rope

Instructions:

Attach the dowel to a wall. It's best to just use removable hooks so you won't have to drill anymore.

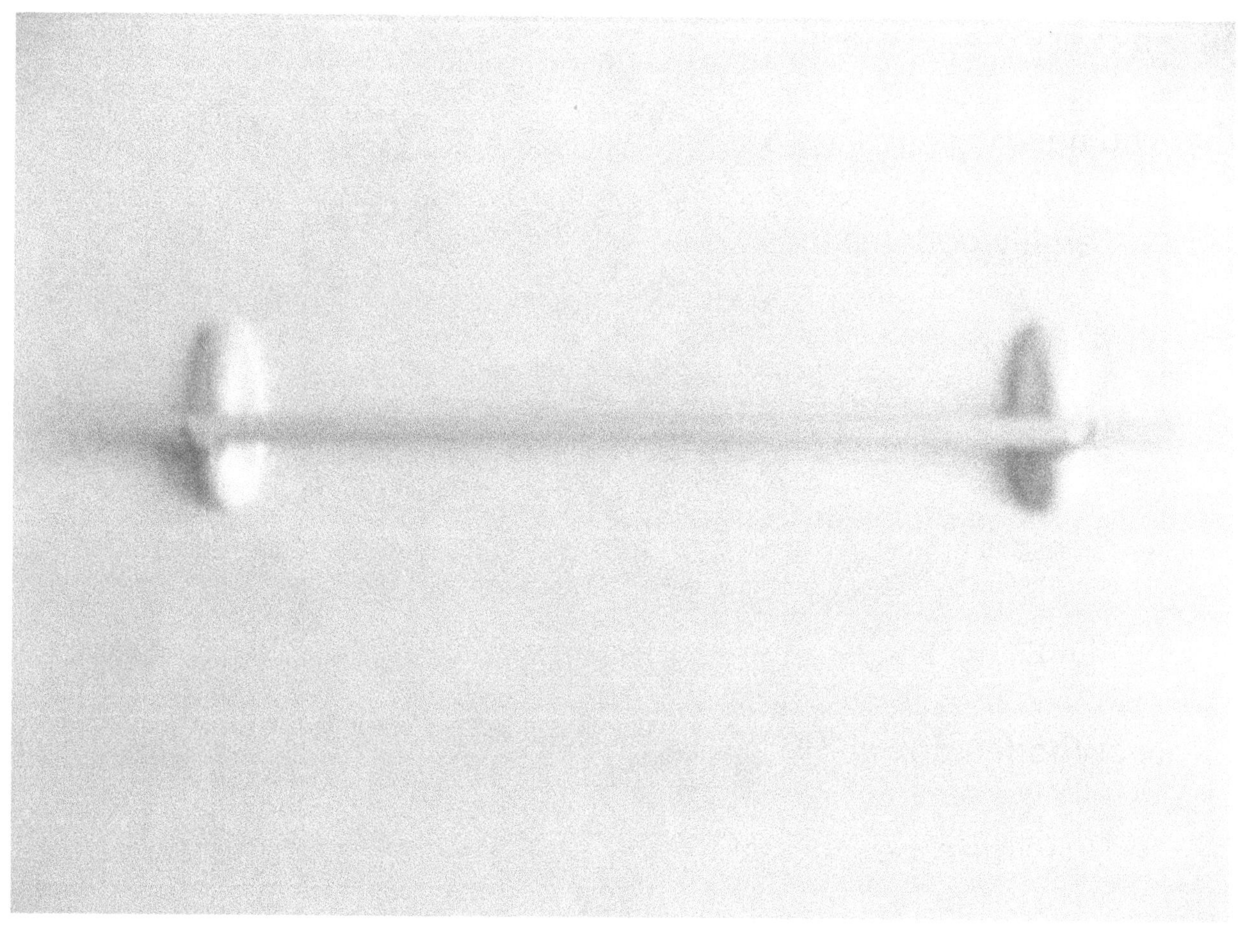

Cut the rope into 14 x 4 pieces, as well as 2 x 5 pieces. Use 5-yard pieces to bookend the dowel with. Continue doing this with the rest of the rope.

Then, start making double half-hitch knots and continue all the way through, like what's shown below.

Once you get to the end of the dowel, tie the knots diagonally so that they wouldn't fall down or unravel in any way. You can also add the wooden beads any way you want, so you'd get the kind of décor that you need. Make sure to tie the knots after doing so.

Use four ropes to make switch knots and keep the décor all the more secure. Tie around 8 of these.

Add a double half hitch and then tie them diagonally once again.

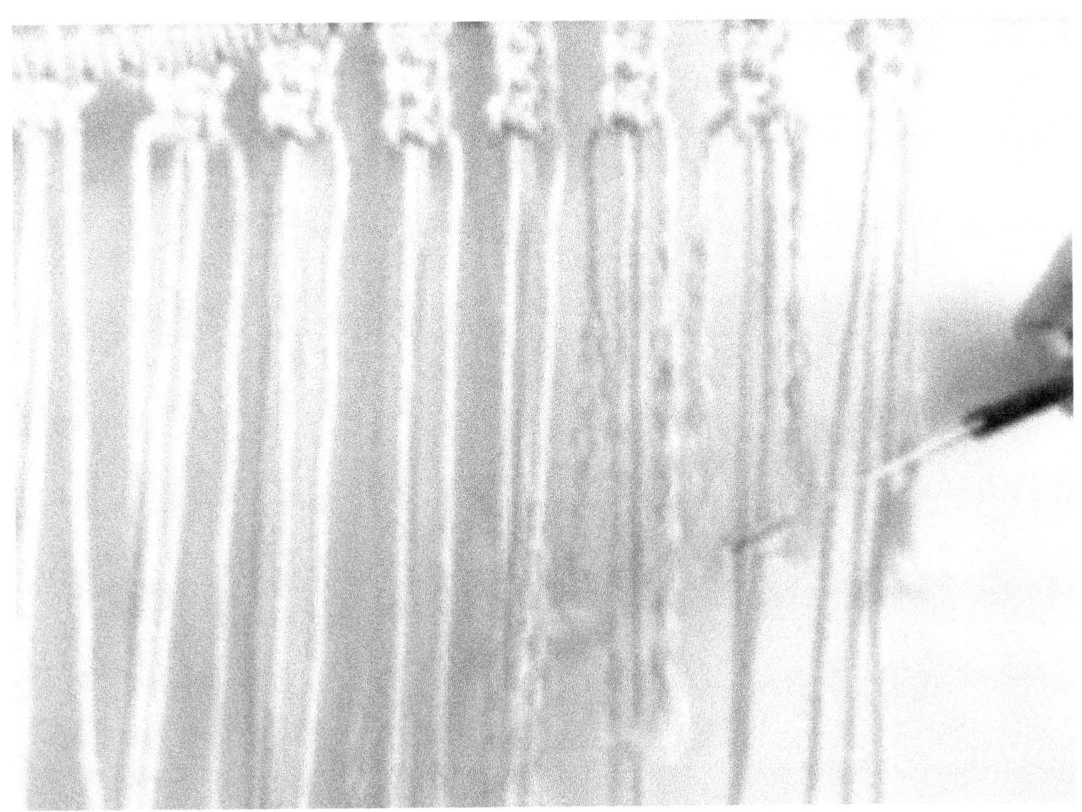

Add more beads and then trim the ends of the rope.

Once you have trimmed the rope, go ahead and add some paint to it. Summery or neon colors would be good.

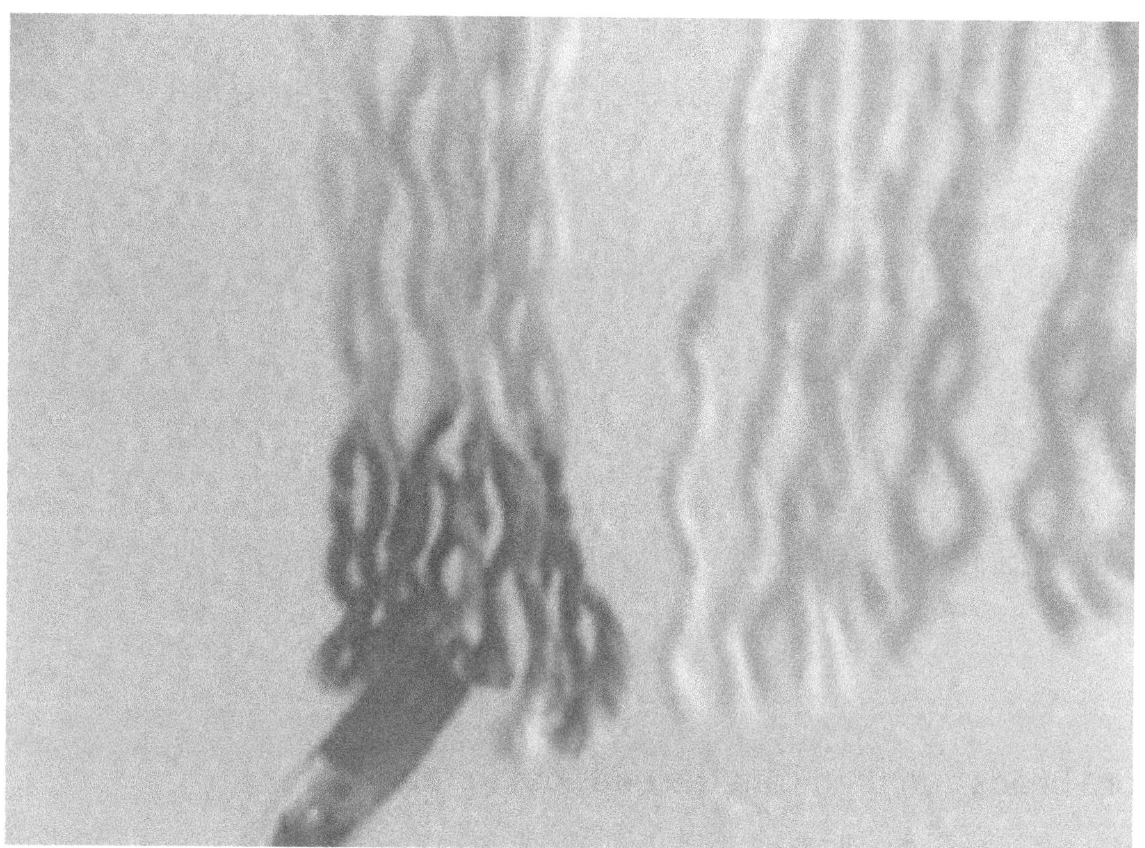

That's it! You now have your own Macramé Wall Art!

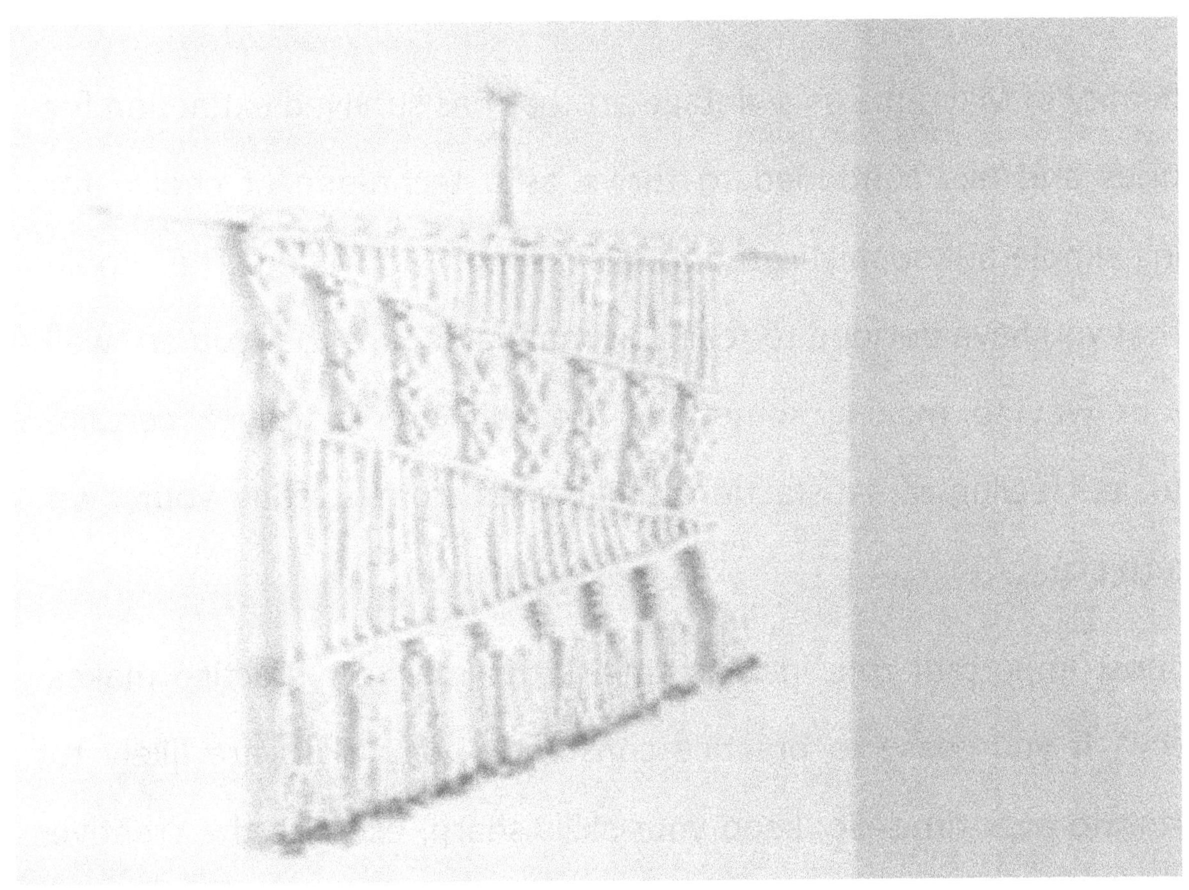

Conclusion

The beauty of Macramé as a vintage art that has survived extinction for centuries and has continued to thrive as a technique of choice for making simple but sophisticated items is simply unrivalled. The simple fact that you have decided to read this manual means that you are well on your way to making something great. There is truly a certain, unequaled feeling of satisfaction that comes from crafting your own masterpiece.

The most important rule in Macramé is the maxim: "Practice makes perfect." If you cease to practice constantly, your skills are likely to deteriorate over time. So, keep your skills sharp, exercise the creative parts of your brain, and keep creating mind-blowing handmade masterpieces. Jewelry and fashion accessories made with even the most basic Macramé knots are always a beauty to behold, hence they serve as perfect gifts for loved ones on special occasions. Presenting a Macramé bracelet to someone, for instance passes the message that you didn't just remember to get them a gift, you also treasure them so much that you chose to invest your time into crafting something unique specially for them too, and trust me, that is a very powerful message. However, the most beautiful thing about Macramé is perhaps the fact that it helps to create durable items. Hence you can keep a piece of decoration, or a fashion accessory you made for yourself for many years, enjoy the value and still feel nostalgic anytime you remember when you made it. It even feels better when you made that item with someone. This feature of durability also makes Macramé accessories incredibly perfect gifts.

Macramé can also serve as an avenue for you to begin your dream small business. After perfecting your Macramé skills, you can conveniently sell your items and get paid well for your products, especially if you can perfectly make items like bracelets that people buy a lot. You could even train people and start your own little company that makes bespoke Macramé fashion accessories. The opportunities that Macramé presents are truly endless.

There you have it, everything you need to know to get you started with your own macramé knots. This is going to show you just how easy it is to get started in this hobby, and once you get the hang of things, you are going to find that it is easier than ever to get started with your own projects.

the [illegible] to create durable [illegible] can keep a piece of

de[illegible] a fashion accessory you [illegible] for yourself for many

[illegible]

CPSIA information can be obtained
at www.ICGtesting.com
Printed in the USA
BVHW011258030921
616012BV00010B/176

9 798670 747479